D0931460

Feminine Soul

Feminine Soul

THE FATE
of an
IDEAL

Marilyn Chapin Massey

BEACON PRESS
Boston

Copyright © 1985 by Marilyn Chapin Massey

Beacon Press books are published under the
auspices of the Unitarian Universalist Association
of Congregations in North America,
25 Beacon Street, Boston, Massachusetts 02108

Printed in the United States of America

(hardcover) 9 8 7 6 5 4 3 2 1

Library of Congress Cataloging in Publication Data

Massey, Marilyn Chapin, 1942–
   Feminine soul.

   Bibliography: p.
   Includes index.
   1. Soul.   2. Woman (Theology)   I. Title.
BL290.M37   1885   305.4'2'01   84–28312
   ISBN 0–8070–6720–2

For Mary Eleanor Chapin, 1911–1972

7-18-85

Contents

Preface

OVER A CENTURY AGO, Hegel, the giant of German idealism, wrote what could be read today as a denial of the most cherished premise of contemporary feminism—the personal is the political. In attempting to describe mankind's embrace of a common and universal good that binds a community and allows for political order, Hegel speculated that "the community only gets an existence through its interference with the happiness of the Family." Using the story of Antigone as his example, he linked women's love in the family with the type of individualism and self-interest that fosters separatism, pits family against family, and prohibits mankind's realization of the universal consciousness necessary for political community. To exist, the community "creates for itself in what it suppresses and what is at the same time essential to it an internal enemy—womankind in general. Womankind—the everlasting irony [in the life of the community]—changes by intrigue the universal end of government into a private end." [1]

This book began a number of years ago in the midst of my studies of the left-wing Hegelians' criticisms of religion, when I came to be fascinated with Hegel's comments on the suppression of womankind and his characterization of it as "the everlasting irony" in mankind's political life. In particular, I began to wonder about the relationship between the left-wing Hegelian charge, made in various ways by D. F. Strauss, Ludwig Feuerbach, Arnold Ruge, and Karl Marx, that the Christianity of the day was an enemy of modern political life and Hegel's charge that womankind was an enemy of political life.

In an earlier book, *Christ Unmasked: The Meaning of "The Life of Jesus" in German Politics,* I made some tentative associations between those two enemies.

At the end of that study, in which I only scratched the surface of German culture and gender ideology, I found I wanted to know more about the relationship between that early nineteenth-century German idealization of the feminine, which approached a deification of womankind, and what has now become a classic criticism of religion as ideology. And I was left with deep suspicions about the usefulness and meaning of that criticism for women's own understanding of religion as an enemy and as a friend.

Another more contemporary characterization of womankind fed my interest—feminists' own affirmation of womankind's difference from mankind. The most radical feminists, most notably French feminists, are making claims about woman's innate and unique morality and spirituality that appear to resurrect the nineteenth-century idealizations of womankind. Today the premise that woman is different vies with the premise that the personal is political, and some feminists come close to claiming that this different womankind is an everlasting irony in mankind's flawed and oppressive political community.

Soon my historical questions about woman and religion in early nineteenth-century German culture began to play with my interest in contemporary feminists' nearly metaphysical or religious claims for womankind. Are there, I wondered, important relationships between the current feminist affirmation of the feminine and the influential heritage of the German criticism of religion?

I began to work my way toward answers in the courses I taught at Harvard Divinity School—courses on the Hegelians and Marx on Christianity, Pietism and romanticism in Germany, and feminist theory. In further study of the left-wing Hegelians, especially of Feuerbach and Marx, I was impressed with how thoroughly their criticisms of religion were permeated by gender imagery, which cannot be dismissed as "mere" metaphor, and thus how intimately their assumptions about gender were bound up with their dismissal of religion as ideology. As I dug in nineteenth-century German Pietism and romanticism, I unearthed what seemed to be a worship of women that rivaled the nineteenth-century Catholic devotion to Mary, which was revived by her appearances in France. And, finally, as I studied contemporary French feminist theory, I found a path back from Lacan and Derrida through Freud and Marx to Hegel and the German romantics. Thus, as I asked questions about the historical and contemporary idealization of woman and the criticism of religion, a plethora of historical and theoretical associations became apparent. My problem became, not how to prove they were there, but how best to present them.

Careful tracking of the trails of association I had found would have required several books but not really the book I wanted to write. What I hoped to do was make these associations come alive outside a chain of ideas in scholars' heads and even outside a particular cultural context, in order to suggest their effects on women's lives and psyches and their significance for women's interpretation of religion.

I was able to discover a way to structure this book with the help of a group of colleagues at the Bunting Institute of Radcliffe College, where I spent a year on a fellowship. There Carolyn Bynum, Linda Gordon, Nancy K. Miller, Ellen Bassuk, and Eve Sedgwick read my work in progress and gave me the opportunity to react in turn to their works of brilliance in religion, social history, French literature, the history of mental health care, and English literature. The interdisciplinary context in which we tested feminist theory and talked about how to study history led me to decide not to work directly with the famous theoretical writings of historical figures like Hegel, Marx, and Freud or with those of contemporary feminists. Rather I have chosen to work with more obscure historical materials that were directly tied to social and political policies and to find in these materials and their fate links to contemporary feminist theory.

There are indeed important relationships between the current feminist affirmation of womankind and the nineteenth-century suppression of womankind that Hegel deemed necessary for mankind's political life. This book is my attempt to describe those relationships and to demonstrate the need for new ways of understanding religion, gender, and ideology.

Acknowledgments

I WOULD LIKE to thank the faculty at Harvard Divinity School for the support and intellectual companionship that enabled me to write this book. I am especially indebted to my colleagues Clarissa Atkinson, Margaret R. Miles, Sharon Welch, Sharon Parks, Nancy Jay, and Constance Buchanan and to the visiting scholars Catherine Prelinger, Sheila Briggs, and Barbara Corrado Pope for their brilliant conversation and writings on women and religion. Harvey Cox and I taught a seminar together on spirituality and politics that contributed energy and ideas to this work. William Hutchinson both listened to and read pieces contributing to the book and I appreciate his concern and his criticisms. Most of all I am indebted to the interest and ideas of students, especially Richard Seager, Susan Bruno, Irma Gonzalez, Mary Condren, and Patricia Gleason. Finally, I am grateful to Harvard University for making me its 1983 nominee to the Bunting Institute of Radcliffe College, where I finished this book.

Feminine Soul

1

Rebirth of the Feminine Soul

*There are two human souls, that is, a masculine soul
and a feminine soul. Thus, woman not only has a soul,
whatever the impertinent [Christian theological]
misogynists may have thought, but she has a soul
essentially different from ours, a soul which is the
inverse of ours, inverse and complementary.* Different
in mind and heart, different *in imagination and character,
intimately and essentially* different *woman brings us
a new spiritual world and not only a more or less
watered down re-edition of the spiritual world of man.*[1]

JEAN ISOULET, *La Cité Moderne*

*The essential and fundamental sin of woman is the
refusal of her femininity!* [2]

HENRY CAFFAREL, *Marriage Is Holy*

*We need to imagine a world in which every woman
is the presiding genius of her own body. In such
a world women will truly create new life,
bringing forth not only children (if and as we choose)
but the visions, and the thinking, necessary to
sustain, console, and alter human existence
—a new relation to the universe.*[3]

ADRIENNE RICH, *Of Woman Born*

As WESTERN THEOLOGIANS and philosophers from the time of Christ to the beginning of the modern age wrote about the existence, capacities, and quality of man's soul, they harbored doubts about woman's soul. They were uncertain whether a female possessed in the same way as a male that essential quality through which finite man could transcend his material existence on earth and unite with the infinite and the immaterial.

In the newly industrialized West of the late eighteenth and early nineteenth century, philosophers and theologians, along with physicians, pedagogues, psychologists, and poets, had ostensibly settled the issue in woman's favor. That woman had a soul and that it was *different* from man's, by virtue of its superior religious nature, was one of the most certain Western beliefs at the dawn of the new age.

That this historically recent belief in women's spiritual supremacy nevertheless oppressed women in the eighteenth and nineteenth centuries and that it continues to oppress women today has been a prominent assumption of those seeking the social, political, and economic equality of women. The historian Sheila Rowbotham describes the negative effects of the belief in the feminine soul on the nineteenth-century Western woman: "[This belief] produced a crop of egg-faced ringleted bonneted fragile girls, which successfully internalized woman's role as the helpless, emotional, hysterical angel in the house and was well suited to the division of labor in capitalist society. . . . [Man] made her into his idea of himself. In her he sought his lost nature." [4] This hysterical angel in the house was well suited, above all, to a division of moral and religious labor. Her soul became the repository of those moral values that were not meaningful or useful outside the home in the conduct of political and economic affairs as well as the repository of those religious attitudes no longer espoused by the self-determining men who conducted those affairs. Her soul also became the norm by which the immorality and lack of spirituality of the lower classes were measured.[5]

The belief in woman's unique and superior spirituality has lasted well into the twentieth century. I learned about it in a marriage manual popular in the 1950s and 1960s. Entitled *Marriage Is Holy,* this manual taught that for males "the universe is an object of science and action . . . something to be studied and conquered." [6] Thus the male's vocation is "one of decision, of undertaking, of realization, of leading," of being the "artisan" of the "concrete order of history and progress." [7] His vocation is to shape and govern a secular world, and therefore, when it comes to religion, he has to "do something of an about-face and learn submission, humility and dependence." [8]

By contrast, according to this manual, a female is "more at home in the sphere of religious values; she is more naturally religious." [9] If the male's vocation is secular, hers is thoroughly religious. It is nothing more or less than to represent the mystery of the infinite to the male. Through her instinct and intuition, which are her distinctive modes of thought, and through her sensitive care of persons, which is her distinctive mode of action, a female is in touch in her body and mind with the eternal, with "the presence of the invisible in the visible." [10] Representing by virtue of this touch the mystery of eternity and the unseen to the male, a female is "not called upon to act, to be seen or to give orders." Rather, her invaluable contribution to history is to attract and inspire the male "from the penumbra" of what is his enlightened secular world.[11] This belief in the vocation of the sexes was summed up in a concise formula: "Man can give himself to an idea, to a cause, to a collectivity; spontaneously, woman can give herself only to a person. Insofar as she is open to the call of a living voice, to the distress of an individual, she is firmly indifferent to the abstract and the collective." [12]

Finally, from this book I learned that there were "many unhappy homes in our slums" in which the exercise of the morality so natural to those women privileged enough to be educated according to the standpoint of the text was "only too evidently impossible" because of the horrible state of life there.[13]

Admittedly, I was given a heavy dose of this version of the feminine soul, but few middle-class women escaped taking some amount of this social medicine. Certainly, we can still see the lingering effects of these dosages in the 1980s in the United States in the enormous appeal of the image of the woman in the penumbra of the history-making man, which is quintessentially illustrated by Nancy Reagan gazing at President Reagan. We can also see the effects of this belief in the political strength of the association between an explicit avowal of religion, opposition to the Equal Rights Amendment, and the desire to prohibit abortion.

In the mid-nineteenth century, Karl Marx wrote what can be read as a prophetic description of the belief in the unique religious qualities of women's feminine soul and its relation to political conservatism. In analyzing his own culture, Marx contended that religion reinforced political conservatism and social oppression; thus the criticism of religion was a prerequisite to social and political change. In powerful political poetry, he wrote that religion is "the heart of a heartless world and the soul of soulless conditions. It is the opium of the people." [14] In his century the criticism of religion spread far, wide, and deep among educated men, but in that same century the middle-class woman was defined as profoundly and naturally religious. It is as if when the middle-class Western man took his politics and economics in his own hands, he outgrew his religious soul and relinquished it to woman. He willingly gave woman what he had come to see as a childish, prescientific, unrealistic religious nature. But he gave it to her, rather than abandoning it altogether, because he wanted to retain access to its conservative qualities. Thus, when man gave woman his religious soul, he gave her, as Christopher Lasch has put it, not only the task of creating a haven in a heartless world but also the task of representing as eternal those aspects of his world he did not want to change.[15]

At this point I might be expected to say that feminists have rejected this idea of the feminine soul. Given the widespread recognition among feminist scholars and activists of the negative effects on women of the belief in the feminine soul and of its association with conservative politics, few would expect feminists to support this belief. Yet today a number of leading feminists do seem to be embracing this idea. Feminists like Adrienne Rich claim that if women would express their unique genius or soul, all social, political, and economic life, and even humans' deepest relations, thoughts, and beliefs, will be changed.[16] It is this claim that forces us to reexamine the concept of the feminine soul in order to grasp its fullest meaning.

This book is about the contemporary claims for woman's unique spiritual qualities and their relation to forgotten dimensions of the historical, eighteenth-century and nineteenth-century claims. It is an attempt to answer the question that anyone struggling for the equality of women cannot help asking: Can an appeal to women's unique spiritual qualities lead to more than a trap? The answer I explore in the following chapters is that it can lead to much more. By examining the writings of the eighteenth and nineteenth centuries in which the concept of the feminine soul was first presented, we can recover meanings of the term and thereby come to understand and appreciate the new theory of religion, gender, and ideology based on this belief.

The Feminist Embrace of the Feminine Soul

In a Different Voice, Carol Gilligan's book about the significance of women's expressions about how they make moral choices, has enjoyed enormous popularity.[17] She contends that women's moral voices provide a humanly essential perspective on morality that has been overlooked by the prominent male theoreticians who have defined the norms of moral development. Whether by recording the discourse of men, as did the ancient Plato, or by charting a path of development by listening to males talk about moral choices, as does the contemporary Lawrence Kohlberg, these theoreticians have failed to hear a different, and equally valid, moral voice. What they *have* heard and defined as normative is an ethic of justice and equality, which manifests itself in the ability to make moral judgments based on an abstract principle of what is right for all people everywhere rather than on a historically contingent and learned ethical tradition. What is often heard in the moral discourse of women is different. Women tend to keep in view the effects of a moral decision on all those whom it touches, on what might be called the network of human relations within which any decision inevitably takes place. Through the voices of women can be heard what Gilligan calls an ethic of care. This ethic, whose principles are responsible relation and nurture, complements the ethic of justice and equality and thus enlarges the dimension of what has been defined as the human moral domain.

Gilligan makes several interesting statements that bear on the issue that always lurks in the background in any discussion of the observed mental and behavioral differences between women and men and on which feminist scholarship has made the most ground. This is the question of the relationship of observed behavioral differences to biological difference. We will look at current feminist premises about this issue more fully below, but here it is important to note that Gilligan does not restrict the capacity for an ethic of care to women. The different voice expressing it can be heard in the moral discourse of men as well. At the same time, she speculates that this perspective may arise from women's oppression and thus be similar to the moral vision of all oppressed groups. In a tentative fashion, she also speculates that this perspective may be linked to women's bodies, that is, to the fact that women bear children. She says, "Rather than viewing [woman's] anatomy as destined to leave her with a scar of inferiority [as does Freud's theory of penis envy], one can see instead how it gives rise to experiences which illumine a reality common to both of the sexes." These experiences are those of childbirth and mothering and this reality is the "reality of connection," of our interdependence on one another, of the truth "that things unseen undergo change through time," and of the awareness "that the boundaries between self and other" are not as sharp as the masculine ideals of autonomy and control of nature define them.[18]

Far more extreme than Gilligan's statements are the claims of contemporary French feminists that women speak a new truth arising from their unique physical experience and that this truth has a significant political meaning. This truth does not complement Western male moral discourse, but instead aims to subvert it and to engender resistance to the multiple global oppressions it has fostered.

In the aptly entitled volume *The Future of Difference*, Domna Stanton explains that for many of these feminists "the act of speaking and, even more, of writing as a female represents a fundamental birth drive which will destroy the old order of death." [19] The old order of death is the order created by the male described in *Marriage Is Holy*, a man who views the universe as "something to be studied and conquered." [20] Rich describes this order as the "death-culture of quantification, abstraction, and the will to power." [21] It is our contemporary Western culture in which man's scientific logic has produced nuclear weapons by which the life of the human species itself can be destroyed, and in which his political and economic logic shapes collectivities in terms of this threat. The French feminist Luce Irigaray claims that only

a way of thinking emerging from women's bodies can transform this death-dealing male thought. She writes, "Woman's [sexual] desire most likely does not speak the same
language as man's desire, and it probably has been covered over by the logic that has dominated the West since
the Greeks." [22] Though accepting Freud's assertion that
the mature male's sexuality is located in the single definitive organ of the penis, these feminists, like Gilligan, refuse to accept his definition of women's sexuality in terms
of the lack of the organ. Since women do not have this
organ, women's sexuality is diffuse and supports a thinking that is comfortable with a continual fluidity of different finite forms. Women's way of thinking does not
seek, therefore, as does male thinking, to measure finite
forms in terms of a single fixed norm of identity. It is
the male preoccupation with this fixed norm of identity
that generates an abstract norm of sameness. Further,
rather than promoting the equality of different peoples,
this norm of identity has, on the contrary, served as the
measure by which those males who possess the privilege
of defining thought as well as the privilege of the organ
have subjugated all those who are different. The French
feminists see class as well as cultural differences between
people as elements in the oppressions perpetrated in the
name of Western man's truth. And they, like Irigaray,
believe that only female self-expression emerging from
woman's different body can transform the global order
of death that men have created in all its current forms.[23]

Finally, Mary Daly in her most recent book, *Pure
Lust*, attempts in her own political poetry to unearth
meanings of words covered over by this Western male
logic. She goes so far as to claim that woman's difference
from man is so deep that the male-defined Western concept of the human species does not apply to her. Like
Irigaray, Daly finds that the concept of the species as defined by male logic represses difference because it reduces
the many to the one and reduces collectivity to an abstraction. A vastly different understanding of species

arises from women's lust, an experience of a unity that generates, rather than represses, difference. Daly writes, "A radical feminist is committed to the Race of women, to our becoming and freedom. Therefore she feels Rage at the oppression of her sisters of all races, of all ethic groups, of all classes, of all nations. She identifies with women as *women*." [24]

The words of Daly and the other feminists quoted above are striking, and inevitably troubling. In tying women's difference as women to ultimate revelations or transformations of human truth and culture, all these feminists make claims that seem to echo those made by Jean Isoulet, the nineteenth-century philosopher cited at the opening of this chapter who believed that women bore the promise of a spiritual world superior to that experienced by and described by men.

Gender, Politics, and Ideology

These claims for women's uniqueness appear to challenge the fundamental premise of contemporary feminism that gender differences are not metaphysical or natural but constructed. As Simone de Beauvoir explained, femininity is woman's second, constructual nature, not her essence. [25] Working from the theory of historical materialism according to Marx and the theories of psychoanalysis according to Freud, feminist scholars have identified gender as a construction, a social and psychic construction tied to material conditions. [26]

In the context of this recent scholarship on gender, the terms *male* and *female* designate relatively stable, if not absolutely clear, differences in biology. The terms *masculine* and *feminine,* by contrast, designate historically contingent interpretations of the meanings of these biological sex differences. In interpreting the meaning of biological difference in relation to its particular social and economic arrangement, each society produces its own specific definitions of masculinity and femininity. Thus, nothing metaphysical or natural can be claimed for the gender ideals of any society; gender is not given with a metaphysical soul or a biological body. The meaning of *masculine* or *feminine* depends on the particular pattern of personal growth determined by a particular historical family or parenting arrangement, which in turn is dependent on the particular social and economic conditions within different societies. There is no intrinsic connection between the female body and the feminine soul. The female body is an identifiable biological entity; the feminine soul is a historically contingent social ideal.

Sheila Rowbotham derived her description of the effects of the belief in the feminine soul on women from this feminist definition of gender. She, in effect contends that the biological difference between female and male was interpreted in the nineteenth century in the West to mean that woman had a soul that enabled her to be the angel in the home of the middle-class nuclear family within the capitalist social and economic arrangement. This soul, then, is a historical idea, an ideology, not an eternal truth.

Using the insights of gender scholarship, Rowbotham characterizes our modern Western ideal of the feminine soul as ideological, in much the same way that Marx identified the religion that oppressed the people in his culture as ideological. For him religion was the correlate of specific conditions of oppression. An illusory set of ideas, defined in its normative form by the dominant class, religion served the interests of that class. Most importantly, it pacified the masses by hiding from them the actual conditions of their lives and their own potential by offering them fulfillment in an imaginary heaven.[27] Rowbotham's interpretation of the belief in the feminine soul parallels Marx's argument. First, she identifies the concept of the feminine soul as merely a contingent historical idea that arose from specific social and material conditions and was then falsely granted the status of an eternal or natural truth. Second, she describes this idea as an illusory projection of male consciousness that serves male interests. Third, she claims that although false and illusory, this idea was a precise and powerful instrument of social control, that is, of the pacification of women.

In light of this important and, indeed, damning analysis of the feminine soul as ideological, how can its once cherished and culturally transformative promise be entertained at all? Yet it is being entertained, and by those feminists who have worked most diligently to identify the illusory and oppressive nature of gender ideas. Even if we make allowances for the obvious and important fact that the most extreme of these feminists, such as Rich, Daly, and Irigaray, are playing with language and using poetry and metaphor as their political parlance, we may still wonder: Are these political poets merely reviving the nineteenth-century ideology of the feminine soul? Are they merely offering us a new religion of woman as the heart of a heartless world? Several writers have grappled with these questions.

In *Contemporary Feminist Thought*, Hester Eisenstein asks these questions and concludes that those feminists who have gone to the extremes of what she calls the women-centered perspective are not politically radical but reactionary. Although she concedes that there is a tradition in Western feminism that has argued for women's rights to full participation in social, economic, and political arenas on the basis of their difference from men, specifically women's superior spiritual qualities, she claims that rights have been and will be won more often on the basis of an argument for women's fundamental equality with men. In her view, the danger that feminists court in making an absolute turn to woman for truth is that they will abandon the heritage of the "three streams" of modern Western liberating social and political theory, which have provided secure bases for the victories women have won in their struggle for equality. These "streams" are the political theory of liberalism itself, which is represented in the work of the Enlightenment philosophers of autonomy and of the social contract, who "contested the divine right of monarchs and aristocrats to political rule"; Marxist socialist theory; and "the strand of social theory that examined the relationship of sexuality to society," which owes a debt to Freud.[28] According to Eisenstein, extreme women-centered feminists are abandoning the very traditions that led to our contemporary liberating theory of gender and to many of our political triumphs as well.

At the root of Eisenstein's criticism is her charge that the most radical proponents of women's difference, such as Rich, the French feminists, and Daly, run the risk of becoming "metaphysical or spiritual" *rather than* "political."[29] She argues that claims for women's difference run the risk of reifying a "feminine" quality, of drawing women into an imaginary world of projected ideals, and of pulling them away from the day-to-day struggle by which rights are gained and lost in the totally secularized political context bequeathed to us by Western liberating theory. These feminists run the risk of offering us a new religion instead of a new politics. To the extent that they embrace a unique spirituality, one might say that they run the risk of finding themselves allied with our contemporary political conservatives, who are quite at home with the superior moral qualities of women. Eisenstein's prescription is that women retain their alliance with those Western liberating traditions that have themselves battled religious belief as a politically conservative force, as an opiate, and as an illusion.

There is no question that a retreat to a private, all-women realm or to the fusion of religion and politics holds its dangers for women. But Eisenstein's assertion of the benefits of the separation of religion and politics is based both on a superficial understanding of religion and on a limited historical understanding of the relationship between religion and politics in the modern era. She therefore misses the import of the new theory of religion, gender, and politics implied in the arguments of the women-centered feminists. In fact, the origin of this new theory is crucial. The dissatisfaction with modern liberating theories and their failure to support women's full participation in Western culture led the contemporary women-centered feminists not only to turn to women's experience, as Eisenstein acknowledges, but also to enlist spirituality in the cause of radical politics.

The Failure of Liberating Theories

The formulators of Western liberating theories did not take adequate account of women's experience and their particular needs for liberation. As a consequence, feminist scholars have recently focused on how Marx's and Freud's theories of social and psychological construction left dimensions of women's experience behind or beneath the historical and psychological processes they described. Through recovering these dimensions of women's experience, women-centered feminists have begun to offer us a fusion of spirituality and politics that questions the liberating potential of Marx's and Freud's theories. In order to appreciate the achievement of these feminists, we should first explore the earlier theories.

Feminists look in vain in Marx's theory for an analysis of the full significance and dynamics of the reproduction of humans. Hilary Rose describes succinctly what Marx did not see: "The production of people is . . . qualitatively different from the production of things." [30] What Marx did see is that the process of the production of things, the potential and conditions of human labor, is the basis for the production of people. That is, he saw the process of the production of things as the process of the construction of human nature itself. Marx held that humans create their own nature (in the sense of human essence) by their transformation through labor of physical nature (in the sense of the natural material world that lies outside and all around humans). Further, human labor is always social because it necessarily involves the

relation of humans to one another in some sort of arrangement of the division of labor; thus the human
nature created through labor is always a social nature.
It is always people in relation to one another and in relation to material conditions.

What Marx did not see clearly is that the production
of people in relation to one another requires women's
bodies, their physical labor, their consciousness, and their
"caring labor—the labor of love." [31] Rose concludes that
in the Marxist tradition "the prioritization of the production process ignores that other materialist necessity of
history—reproduction. The preoccupation with production as a social process with a corresponding social division of labor and the neglect of reproduction as an
analogous process with its division of labor perpetuates
a one-sided materialism." [32]

Marx's failure to take sufficient account of any of the
elements of the production of people in relation to wom-
en's bodies in his description of how the human con-
structs its nature and its gender ideals is manifest at many
points in the theory of historical materialism. The most
crucial point for us is Marx's position on physical nature
itself. He wrote, "Labour is, in the first place, a process
in which both Man [i.e., the human species] and Nature
participate, and in which man of his own accord starts,
regulates, and controls the material relations between
himself and Nature. He opposes himself to Nature as
one of her own forces, setting in motion arms and legs,
heads and hands, the natural forces of his body in order
to appropriate Nature's productions in a form adopted
to his wants. By thus acting on the external world and
changing it, he at the same time changes his own nature." [33]

Here there is no talk of those natural forces of the
body that have traditionally been viewed as cooperating
with nature, the forces of women's body necessary for the
production of people, or of their contribution to the social
nature of humans. There is, rather, the familiar talk of

opposition to, appropriation of, and control of nature. Isaac Balbus asks the question many feminists have asked of this view of the relation of the human to physical nature: "Is it not possible . . . that the definition of production as *the* distinctively human activity participates in the characteristically male denigration of the nonproductive activities to which women have been historically disproportionately consigned?" [34] By this question, Balbus clearly defines the failure of historical materialism to account for woman's experience.

Just as Marx's theory of historical materialism reveals more than a simple omission of the experience of women, so Freud's theory of the psychological construction of gender identity as illustrated in the Oedipus myth reveals a perspective antithetical to woman's experience. Once dismissed as a defense for the bourgeois nuclear family, this theory is now being reinterpreted by feminists to mean that sexual identity is only attained through a process of struggle within the family; that is, sexual identity is constructed. Moreover, they find it valuable for highlighting precisely those intimate physical and familial experiences that Marxist theory passes over. Attempts to blend the insights of psychoanalysis and Marxism in order to extend the range of materialism to include women's bodies, on the one hand, and to historicize the process of the construction of sexual identity, on the other, have arisen from the explorations of the shortcomings in both theories. As familiar as the Oedipal theory may be to some readers, I will retell it here in some detail not only because each retelling produces a wonder that it was believed but also because its themes are crucial to understanding the claims of the women-centered feminists.

Freud tells us that the "child's first erotic object is the mother's breast that nourishes it; love has its origin in attachment to the satisfied need for nourishment." [35] At first the child "does not distinguish between the breast and its own body," but gradually it learns that its mother is a separate being. When it does so it yearns for unity with her. And the mother "by her care of the child's body . . . becomes its first seducer." [36] Thus a mother's nurture and care are the occasions for the child's first erotic experiences. The early relation to the mother becomes "the prototype" or the original model "of all later love-relations—for both sexes." [37]

Freud then tells us that when the boy child at age two or three begins to locate erotic pleasure in his sexual organ, he "becomes his mother's lover." He wants to "possess her physically" the way his father does in sexual intercourse. He wants to be his father, to take his place. It is important to note that even before he covets the father's sexual privileges with the mother, the father has "been an envied model to the boy, owing to the physical strength he perceives in him and the authority with which he finds him clothed." [38] But despite all this admiration, the boy child wants to kill his father in order to take his sexual place with the mother.

The child is prohibited by the castration complex. To check the son's inappropriate desire, the mother threatens the boy with the loss of his penis. In fact, to reinforce her threat she tells him that it is his father who will cut it off. But even this reinforced threat would have no effect if the boy did not at some time see the female genitals, "which really lack this supremely valued part." [39] Only then does he believe the reality of castration. A "normal" male heterosexuality develops when the little boy, believing this threat is real, represses his desire for his mother and respects his father's sexual role. Identifying with the father, he will grow up to someday possess, as the father does, a woman like the mother.

Balbus points out that this struggle for male heterosexuality produces the gender characteristics that we in the modern West consider to be masculine. Notice that it also produces what Gilligan calls the Western male ethic of justice and equality and a version of Marx's man as laborer. Balbus writes, "Because the father is so powerful, and so frightening, his internalization produces a particularly harsh superego, leaving the male child with a highly developed conscience. This conscience, in turn, serves as the basis of the sense of justice and social obligation without which civilization would be impossible. At the same time, the male child's powerful superego enables him to sublimate his sexual energies in the form of labor that is equally indispensable for civilization. Becoming a man means learning to defer his desire for a woman; masculinity entails the capacity to postpone gratification." [40]

Using the Oedipus complex to produce femininity obviously presented theoretical problems to Freud and indescribable real problems for women treated by psychoanalytical practice. Freud's own words are indispensable here: "A female child has, of course, no need to fear the loss of the penis; she must, however, react to the fact of not having received one. From the very first she envies boys its possession; her whole development may be said to take place under the colors of envy for the penis. She begins by making vain attempts to do the same as boys and later, with greater success, makes efforts to compensate for her defect—efforts which may lead in the end to a normal feminine attitude." [41] What she does is learn to repress her love for her mother by resenting her for lacking a penis. She learns to transfer her love to the father, to identify herself with her lacking mother, and like the mother to have the father's penis "at her disposal" in sexual intercourse. But then she goes on to learn from all this lack an even better lesson. She learns to substitute a wish for a baby for the wish for a penis.[42] The price women pay for accepting the Freudian construction of gender identity is high indeed.

Rich has described this price as accepting a belief that "the two-person mother-child relationship is by nature regressive, circular, unproductive, and that culture depends on the father-son relationship." [43] In various reinterpretations of what is called the pre-Oedipal period of human development, which is characterized by the mother-child dyadic relation, feminists have demonstrated that they are not willing to pay the price.[44]

Rich goes still further and raises the basic question posed by feminists about both Marx's and Freud's treatments of reproduction and the mother: "Can the mother, in patriarchy, represent culture?"[45] The answer given by Rich, Daly, and the French feminists is, in one sense, the now classic one that de Beauvoir gave in *The Second Sex.* No, in patriarchy, the mother cannot represent culture but only the stasis of nature and the danger of regression. But these women-centered feminists do not stop at this point; they go on to say something new. They say that when woman's body is freed from patriarchy, from its myth and institutions, woman's body can express, represent, and bring about a new culture. Rich writes, "In arguing that we have by no means yet explored or understood our biological grounding, the miracle and paradox of the female body and its spiritual and political meanings, I am really asking whether women cannot begin, at last, to *think through the body,* to connect what has been so cruelly disorganized."[46] Rich is asking women to connect their powers of mind with their own complex range of physical experience.

Rich and other feminists are posing a new challenge, one that asks women to reform their self-perception in such a way that they have a wholeness of spirit and body. In this study I will show that in posing questions like this for woman, feminists are not divorcing spirituality and politics, but offering a new interpretation of religion, gender, and ideology that has radical political implications. In the process they are recovering a knowledge about woman's transformative cultural potential that at times was carried by the premodern belief in the feminine soul but was suppressed in the production of our Western liberation theories. The goal of awareness described by Rich transcends the goals of other feminists who are still committed to a belief in the power of the liberating theories of the West. These feminists hold that liberation must come through these Western traditions. For example, Eisenstein proposes a type of fusion of the women-centered perspective with feminism's intellectual and political heritage as "the chief work of feminist theory and practice for the foreseeable future." [47] She writes, "From a theoretical point of view, [this] means associating feminism with the liberating traditions of Western thought, from Rousseau to Marx and Engels, tending in the direction of greater equality, shared decision-making, and justice. But it means, too, transforming those traditions, by imbuing them with the woman-centered values of nurturance and intimacy, as necessary and legitimate goals of political life." [48] Eisenstein contends that in turning their backs on these liberating traditions in order to affirm woman's unique experience and its visions, the women-centered extremists are divorcing spirituality from politics rather than performing the necessary task of integration.

What Eisenstein does not recognize is that in the very formation of the liberating traditions of Western thought she singled out from Rousseau to Marx and Engels, and on to Freud as well, the political potential of the values of nurture and intimacy were suppressed. Moreover, she does not see that it is not the contemporary women-centered feminists who have divorced spirituality from politics; rather this separation was made by the giants of the liberating traditions themselves. To illustrate this claim, I will chart a history of failed attempts to imbue, as Eisenstein suggests, liberating traditions "with the woman-centered values of nurturance and intimacy, as necessary and legitimate goals of political life." [49] On the basis of that history we will be able to see that the new embrace of a feminine soul represents not the return to an old ideology, but a new theory of ideology and of religion that has radical, not reactionary, political meaning.

The liberating theories Eisenstein describes were criticisms of religion; they viewed the divorce of a certain type of spirituality from politics as essential to man's gaining freedom. The religion they criticized was the culturally dominant religion of Christianity, a religion imaged in terms of the relationship of God the father and his divine and human sons. The type of spirituality that had to be divorced from politics in order for man to gain his freedom was the type that fostered a childlike dependence of sons on the authority and power of God the father and his earthly political representatives. The philosophers of autonomy and of the social contract thus criticized the divine revelation that infantilized man's mind and God the father's earthly representatives in politics—divinely ordained kings and priests who kept man dependent on their authority.

Many of the philosophers of autonomy were willing to retain the reality of God and even Christianity so long as the adult/child dynamic of religion was neutralized— at least for men. But Marx and Freud, the two critics of religion who most influenced social scientific theory, both declared in their own ways that the God the father in whom the soul of Western man had sought its destiny and truth was an illusion. Marx's potent description of religion as the heart of the heartless world was written in his introduction to a criticism of Hegel's philosophy of right, which Marx read as an apology for the divine right of monarchs. To him, Hegel's theory of the monarchy was nothing more than the replication in political theory of the Christian doctrine of God's incarnation in Christ, his son.[50] Freud's most potent criticism of religion is found in *Totem and Taboo,* where he locates the origin of belief in God the father in an actual primordial murder of the father by sons seeking possession of the mother.[51]

Thus all the modern liberation theories, in one way or another, associated man's freedom with a recognition that the dominant Western Christian religious discourse, which had for centuries given him definite sociopsychic meanings and secure directives to salvation, was either in part or in whole illusory and exploitative. To be free, man must see that some, if not all, of his religious beliefs are mere ideas, products of his imagination that misplace and misidentify his own human potential for shaping his world.

The heritage of the critique of religion as ideology that pervades Western liberating theory helped feminists see that the woman's soul defined and confirmed in the nineteenth century was similarly a mere idea, a product of human, indeed of male, imagination, an idea that misplaces and misidentifies the true referent of women's cultural potential and serves to legitimate male domination. There can be no doubt that belief in the feminine soul as it was then defined was an instrument of social control of women, serving the interests of male domination in the Western bourgeois society.

Moreover, according to Mary Daly, within Christianity itself this belief functioned primarily to encourage Christian woman's identification with Jesus as a sacrificial victim and to promote the interiorization of his virtues of powerlessness, of "sacrificial love, passive acceptance of suffering, humility, meekness," and, of course, obedience.[52] This belief encouraged men to write marriage manuals like *Marriage Is Holy* and women to believe their words. It encouraged even Christian man to give woman his no longer meaningful or useful childlike religious soul and the function of representing his lost nature.

The oppressive experience of soulful Christian women has evoked from Daly and many others a critique of Western religion similar to that of Marx and Freud. It has evoked multiple exposures of God the father as an illusion, a projection of male imagination, a falsely universalized product of historically specific social conditions, and a tool of social control.[53] Since the women-centered feminists recognize clearly the dangers inherent in speaking of a feminine soul and in encouraging belief in a

tradition opposed to women's freedom, we must question
carefully the content intended by the use of the term
feminine soul in this book.

The Origin of the Feminine Soul

The nineteenth century in the West was marked not only
by the confirmation of woman's soul but also by the appearance of new heretical religious discourses that called
into question the truth of the Christian system of salvation through the relations of God the father and his son
as profoundly as did the criticisms of the liberating the-
orists. This heretical discourse posed its challenge by
imaging God in the likeness of the feminine soul. Fifty
years before Marx wrote his famous statement on religion
as the opiate of the masses, the German romantic poet
Novalis declared that the Philistines of his age used religion as an opiate to assuage the pains of everyday life
and to assure themselves a future in heaven commensu-
rate with their desired social status on earth.[54] But in
contrast to Marx, Novalis sought to detoxify his contemporaries, not by abolishing religion and exposing it
as false consciousness, but by creating a new religion. Convinced that rather than serving to ensure social and political stasis, religion could engender a sense of alienation
from given conditions and create the possibilities for
their transformation, Novalis set out to create this new
religion. And woman as a lover and as a mother became
its deity.

　　The genesis and fate of the type of religious knowledge espoused by Novalis, in which belief in the feminine
soul was correlated with belief in God as female, is an
important and generally overlooked aspect of the belief
in the feminine soul. In this religious knowledge, belief
in the unique qualities of the feminine soul extended
beyond an idealization and sentimentalizing of the religious, spiritual, and moral nature of woman to a recon-

ceptualization of the deity itself as female and powerful. The images of this religion were those of mother and child, woman and lover, rather than those of father and son. Furthermore, the nature of the reality created and sustained by this female deity was radically different from the reality believed to be created and sustained by God the father. Strikingly similar to the reality contemporary feminists find heralded by the transformative potential of the feminine soul, this new reality is marked by the continual fluidity of finite forms, the experience of a unity that generates, rather than represses, difference, and the primordial truth of nurture.

Why was this religious knowledge of a female God forgotten and only the constraining knowledge of a feminine soul remembered from the nineteenth century? To understand the new theory of religion, gender, and ideology offered by contemporary women-centered feminists, we must be able to answer this historical question and, more importantly, to see the relation of the loss of this religious knowledge to Western liberating traditions.[55] In order to explain why feminists who are fully aware of the oppressive force of the heritage of ideas about woman's unique feminine soul nonetheless find a transformative potential in it, we need to recover this recent religious knowledge. There are innumerable ways we could do this; many histories of belief in the feminine soul in postmedieval Western history could be written. I shall present one history, and it is a "local" one at that.[56] It will begin at a historical point Rich associates in *Of Woman Born* with the violence of the contemporary institutionalization of motherhood—the widespread infanticide in eighteenth-century Germany[57]—and it will end in the same country with a mid-nineteenth century governmental ban on the establishment of kindergartens. By focusing on local policies and practices that had direct effects on women's bodies, rather than glimpsing events in swatches of geographical space and time, this history of the feminine soul will attempt to recover a religious memory within a context that will allow us to make discoveries about religion and ideology.

Let me make clear at the outset my reasons for using the German context. First, I am using it because it is the one I know. Happily, it has particular resonances with the thought of Marx and Freud. But a "local" history could be entered elsewhere at many points in the space and time of the postmedieval West. The "universals" that would link these local histories are women's bodies, the type of constraints imposed in a modern industrial society, and the ideal of a feminine soul. Second, I am using the German context to provide me with culturally influential tales told by men about moral and religious development. Again such tales can be found in many contexts of the postmedieval West. Some of them would not have the same immediacy of relation to the thought of Marx and Freud as the ones I have chosen but they would still most likely have an immediacy of relation to another strand of liberating theory. I am not interested in making a particular argument about the function of the ideology of the feminine soul in German history and its relation to Germany's militarism and tragic national history. Again, such a history might be written. My interest is in opening up, through one local history, questions about the relation between women's bodies and the modern ideal of the feminine soul.

I will present my local history through the narration and explication of three tales and their fate at the hands of contemporary thinkers. The three tales are *Leonard and Gertrude,* written by Johann Heinrich Pestalozzi, the father of modern German pedagogy; *Henry of Ofterdingen,* written by the poet Novalis, one of the founding fathers of German romanticism; and *Mother and Play Songs,* written by Friedrich Froebel, the founder of the kindergarten system. In each of these tales the feminine soul figures prominently, so prominently that the divine referent of human moral and religious de-

velopment becomes a female God. These tales were written by men about the *contemporary* moral and religious
development necessary if man were to participate more
fully in determining the conditions of his political and
economic life than he had in his religious and feudal
past. Thus these tales were considered in the context of
their times politically liberal and even radical; they belong on the "left" of the political spectrum. Finally, these
tales, written by authors who are considered founding
fathers of aspects of nineteenth-century German culture,
were appropriated by progressive cultural leaders in Germany and became part of their theories and practices.

This appropriation did not occur without a struggle.
The progressive men who embraced the tales suppressed
their religious meanings, religious meanings of the feminine soul. To do so, these progressive men called on an
ancient tale of moral and religious development that was
first told in the biblical account of the fall of Adam and
Eve in the Garden of Eden; to make our history complete, we shall review this tale as part of the fate of the
German tales. Although progressive and enlightened men
criticized this fundamental Christian tale for its mythic
character and for its negative view of human nature,
they nonetheless returned to it again and again to censor
and suppress religious meanings of the feminine soul.

There is evidence that each of the three German
tales that will be retold inspired women to seek liberation
—a more powerful role within the family, a rebellion
against the family and marriage itself, a freedom to write,
and a demand for participation in social and political
institutions. The liberating potential of the tales is obvious. Rather than focusing on that, this study will attend
to their religious meanings and the subsequent suppression of those meanings. That suppression has a single
theme: the suppression of the religious powers of woman
in favor of the powers of the autonomous ego of man by
which he could determine his historical fate and control
nature. In the descriptions in the tales of the religious

powers of woman, revealed by belief in the feminine soul, we will uncover the threads of the story of human development feminists have found missing in Marx's and Freud's accounts of human self-construction. In these tales we find the threads of the story of the potential of woman's body, her physical labor, her consciousness, and her "caring labor—the labor of love." [58] And we find threads of a different story of the meaning of the mother's body and of the child's separation from it.

Through this local history I will show that there is a relation between the contemporary feminists' ideal of a unique female spirituality and their dissatisfaction with Western liberating theory. The embrace of the ideal of a unique female genius or soul is not merely the resurrection of a historical male ideal, but rather the manifestation of a new perspective on the meanings and effects of this ideal as an ideology and on the liberating theories of the preceding centuries.

In order to develop this new perspective for the reader, I will present the tales describing the feminine soul through what might be called a strategy of narration rather than any statement of principles about ideology. Throughout this book I will use the term *feminine soul* to refer both to the object of a historical belief and to the genius of women about which radical feminists write. By using the term in both contexts, we keep in the forefront the question whether the contemporary women-centered feminists are clinging to an old male illusion or not. Further, by stretching the metaphor of the feminine soul, we also remain aware that the interpretation of the referent of belief in the feminine soul is complex and that our customary ways of interpreting ideology tend to reduce that complexity.

Often, in both historical and contemporary contexts, I will use the term *feminine soul* as if I believed in it, that is, as if the term referred to something real. In doing this, I do not mean to affirm the existence of a feminine soul in the traditional metaphysical sense as an eternal, transhistorical essence of woman. To do so would be merely to confirm the belief held by those men who lauded it. Rather, I mean to reclaim the term for its original meaning as defined by Novalis and others. To do this means to defy centuries of previous Western Christian theology, which only reluctantly affirmed the existence of woman's soul, and then defined it as the same as or a defective version of man's soul.

Though I do not mean to grant a metaphysical reality to the feminine soul, I want to resist identifying it as merely an illusory ideal. To say that belief in this soul is a mere illusion is not to say enough. Whatever its truth value may be, the ideal of the feminine soul, in the past and in the present, has effects. For example, in the past it contributed to what Rowbotham calls woman's successful internalization of her role as a good angel in the middle-class home. In that sense, the feminine soul has its referent in that all too real female internalization of oppressive social ideals of the feminine. Is that the only referent it had in the past? Is that the referent it has today when feminists themselves laud it? We will find that the answer is no. To do this, we must constantly shift our attention from the merely illusory nature of ideas about the qualities of female interiority to their social effects.[59]

In addition, by writing in affirmation of the belief in the feminine soul throughout this study, I can focus on the centrality of exemplary spirituality in the modern ideals of the feminine. Spirituality is the quality of the feminine soul that women have been most reluctant to relinquish as male illusion and that they seem to be resurrecting today. To treat the spirituality of the feminine soul as though it referred to something real allows us to consider the social effect of religious ideas rather than to assume, as did many of the founders of liberating theory, a correlation between their illusory nature and social oppression. In this context, we can pose the question, Does the feminine soul as a religious ideal serve unequivocally as an instrument of the social control of women? Or is the belief now embraced by feminists a new and different religious ideal bearing the promise of resistance to social control and perhaps even radical cultural transformation?

It is important to pry open the ideological analysis of gender ideals because no other set of ideas makes it more evident to us that ideology can have a life of its own, independent of material conditions. It has been of enormous importance for women to realize that different societies have different gender ideals and to formulate in analytical terms the relation of those ideals to material conditions in other societies, and it is equally important to realize that the ideals of women's unique spiritual character have survived a century of dramatic alterations in all dimensions of Western culture. These ideals have even survived in socialist countries, where the capitalist conditions Rowbotham describes do not exist. Because these gender ideals have lasted through economic, social, and political change, feminists have come to see, as Biddy Martin puts it, that struggles "over the production, distribution and transformation of meaning" are at least as crucial as "struggles over economic and political power." [60] This is what Daly, Rich, and the French feminists have come to see and this is why they are concerned with transforming thinking understood as "the generative system which determined the production of meaning." [61] They have come to see that ideas themselves have a material power of their own, and this power cannot be directly equated with or reduced to specific material conditions. They have come to see this by seeing that ideas about woman's unique spiritual qualities have lived on and exert power over women's bodies in socialist countries as well as in capitalist countries.

Their recognition of the material power of ideas over women's bodies led radical women-centered feminists like Rich and Daly and the French feminists to look into the gaps in the theories of Marx and Freud and to rethink the analysis of gender ideals as ideological.

They have begun to reinterpret religious ideals as ideological as well. As a result, they offer us a fresh theory of religion, gender, and ideology. To demonstrate the importance of that reinterpretation, we will examine in a local history the struggle over the production of the ideas of our Western liberation theories. We now enter not only a criticism of religious ideas but also a struggle between different religious ideas, between traditional Christian ideals and those inspired by the feminine soul. That ideological struggle was at the same time a struggle to constrain women's bodies, and so we begin in the thick of German biopolitics with the genesis of concrete policies to constrain women's bodies with the ideal of the feminine soul.

2

Biopolitics and the Birth of the Feminine Soul

Infanticide! Do I dream or am I awake? Is it possible this deed? Does it happen? Does the unnamed happen? No, not the unnamed, the unnamed crime which has found expression in words. Conceal thy face, O Century! Bow down, O Europe! [1]

JOHANN HEINRICH PESTALOZZI, *Germany, 1793*

The soul is the prison of the body. [2]

MICHEL FOUCAULT, *Discipline and Punish*

IN GERMANY BELIEF IN the unique and religiously superior feminine soul was born in the context of the development of modern biopolitics designed to ensure the health
of the German population; this was a politics designed
by men for the control of women's bodies. Ideals of the
feminine soul quickly were conceived in Germany as a
prison for the female body, to bind it to the processes of
reproduction and nurture of children within marriage. It
is no wonder that Simone de Beauvoir declared, "The
eternal feminine is a lie." [3]

De Beauvoir reminds us that it was Germany's
greatest poet, Goethe, who gave the most famous praise
to the eternal feminine. In *Faust* the strains of the mystical chorus leading Faust's soul to heaven chant, "The
eternal feminine beckons us upward." [4] And Adrienne
Rich reminds us that the soul of Faust's earthly lover,
Gretchen, who most clearly represents the eternal feminine for him on his heavenly journey, was the soul of
an infanticide, of a woman who murdered her baby.[5]
Gretchen's soul is there in heaven to beckon Faust's because she paid the price for her crime. After suffering
horrors of regret and repentance, she endured punishment by decapitation.

Goethe's Gretchen was not a mere figment of his
imagination. As Rich also reminds us, infanticide was a
major crime in Germany in the eighteenth century.
Toward the end of that century the writer and educational reformer Pestalozzi answered his own tortured
question—"Infanticide! . . . Does it happen?"—with the
words "My children are killed by the thousands at the
hands of those who give birth to them." Yet he bemoaned
that the sword of justice fell on many of these mothers
during his time.[6]

During the first half of the eighteenth century, a
sixteenth-century code still governed the punishment of
infanticide. According to this code, not only infanticide
but also the concealment of pregnancy and clandestine
childbirth were punishable by public and torturous execution. In his book *Discipline and Punish,* Michel Fou-

cault calls these public executions, which were common for centuries in Christian Europe, theaters of hell because they were intended to prevent crime by instilling the fear of hell in those who watched the horrors inflicted on the criminal. Related to the practice of disciplining the people by theaters of hell, which was carried out with the approval of both the Catholic and Reformed churches, was the theory of matching the horror of the punishment with the prevalence, rather than the nature, of the crime. If we take the degree of torture prescribed for infanticides as a gauge of the prevalence of the crime, we must conclude that this crime was widespread. Live burial, impalement, or sacking and drowning preceded by the tearing of flesh with glowing tongs were the standard punishments. Decapitation by the sword, to which Pestalozzi referred and which Gretchen experienced, was a late amelioration of the prescribed punishments.

Throughout the eighteenth century, enlightened European reformers criticized the severity of the punishments and their efficacy in preventing crimes. At the same time the definition of the female gender began to change, and descriptions of the uniquely religious feminine soul of women began to be formulated. In Germany promotion of the new ideal of the innately strong and good feminine soul replaced theaters of hell as the essential element in a campaign to eliminate infanticide. Praising the qualities of this soul also became the key strategy in programs of humanitarian social reform directed at the more general problem of the lack of proper mothering. Before looking in more detail at what is clearly a strategy for disciplining women by imposing on them ideas of a feminine soul, let us look at how men saw the problems of infanticide and poor mothering.

The Problem of Infanticide

Concern about infanticide was widespread in eighteenth-century Germany. Because it was common in Prussia,

Frederick William I, the father of the reformer Frederick
the Great, issued an edict in 1720 in which he decreed
that sacking be reinstated as the punishment for infanticide in place of what had come to be the common practice, decapitation. The edict read, "Since, we are sorry to
say, experience proves that this crime is becoming all too
common, and many children born out of marriage are
killed at birth by their wicked mothers, and since the
blood of these children cries for revenge, we should attempt to frighten these dissolute minds." [7]

Frederick the Great took a different approach to the
problem and determined to eliminate it rather than
merely punish the criminals. He made several changes in
the law according to two widely held principles of criminal reform: first, "that it would be better to seek out
causes and prevent crimes than to punish them" and,
second, that "natural equity demands that there should
be proportion between the crime and its punishment." [8]

In accordance with the first principle, he inquired
into the social and economic causes of the crime and what
we would call the psychological causes. One of his more
surprising conclusions was that the attitude of the Christian churches, which in his territory meant predominantly
the Lutheran church, was a principle cause of the crime.
As a result of this finding, he opposed the severity of the
punishments prescribed by the churches and in 1746
abolished all public church penances for "sins of the
flesh" because he believed that they had an adverse effect
on the souls of those subjected to public humiliation.
He reasoned that even the fear of public disgrace for sins
of passion gave "occasion for infanticide ... [and served
to] increase resentment and bitterness [rather than] to
produce betterment." [9]

The initial conclusions of his study led Frederick to
wonder whether the laws against infanticide themselves
contributed to the crime. He wrote, "The laws, do they
not attach infamy to clandestine child-birth? A girl only
too easily fooled by the promises of a *seducer,* does she

not find herself compelled by the very force of circumstances, to choose between the loss of her honor [to say nothing of her life] and the elimination of the unhappy fruit that she has conceived?" [10] Anticipating a theme that will be repeated over and over again by later reformers, Frederick contended that the severity of the laws robbed "the state of two subjects, the child which it forces the mother to kill, and then the mother herself in expiation of her crime, a mother who may have intended to make it possible to repair her loss by becoming a legal mother and then to propagate legally." [11]

Even with his enlightened analysis of the oppressive force of laws governing the conditions of childbirth, Frederick still sought to solve the problem only by means of a legal institution, marriage, which in turn legalizes motherhood. He held that reinforcing and expanding control over the institution of motherhood would prevent infanticide. Through changes in the marriage laws, he tried to eliminate what he had discovered to be a major social cause of infanticide—the "seduction" of young women by soldiers, who were forbidden by law from marrying. In order to extend the social breadth of the institution of marriage, he lifted the ban on soldiers' marriages, with the justification that soldiers would fight all the more valiantly if they were defending their own blood in the blood of their children. Furthermore, he criticized the strictness of ecclesiastical marriage laws. Thus Frederick's principal strategy in the campaign to prevent infanticide was the promotion of more marriages and of the status of marriage itself as a social institution essential to the security of the state. Yet despite his efforts, in 1777 he wrote that most of the criminals executed in Prussia were still "girls who killed their infants." [12]

In addition to changing the marriage laws, Frederick introduced other changes in the law that ultimately posed new problems for reformers. Frederick abolished all punishment for any unmarried woman who reported her pregnancy to local authorities or to her employers. This salutary act meant officials now had to deal with these women in a new context. Many of the unmarried mothers who reported their pregnancy and escaped execution under the new laws were offered employment as wet nurses as a means of supporting their children, and welfare systems were even established to provide for the delivery of the children of unmarried mothers. Those who supported the new scheme did so for different reasons. In Hamburg, for example, the institutionalization of wet-nursing was undertaken by groups of men not only as a service for the unmarried women but also as a means for fathers to ensure that their own children received healthy milk.

This humanitarian practice turned out to be a Catch-22 for women and another version of the same problem for reformers. The reformers soon came to see the practice of wet-nursing, which kept poor unmarried mothers from committing infanticide, as a means of genteel, upper-class infanticide. Children given to wet nurses and the wet nurses' own children suffered high mortality rates. Johann Peter Frank, who was a leading advocate for a state agency for the protection of the health of the population, claimed that the practice of wet-nursing was responsible for the complete depopulation of villages.[13]

Faced with the unsatisfactory results of the initial reforms, the reformers took another step. In France, Rousseau, the theoretician of the social contract, drew attention to the social and political significance of breast-feeding by natural mothers rather than wet nurses. He contended that if wet-nursing could be eliminated, if natural mothers would breast-feed their children, morals would be reformed: "Natural feelings will revive in every heart; the state will be repopulated; this first step alone will reunite everybody." [14] Breast-feeding by natural and legal mothers, it seems, was as essential to the social contract as freedom of the will.

In Germany, Frank not only echoed these opinions in his book *System of a Complete Medical Police,* he also linked them to infanticide. He wrote the enormously important words, "If one hopes to protect the rights of man, then mothers must no longer be permitted to treat their children as barbarously as they please." [15] He argued for laws to force "mothers to conduct themselves in ways which benefit both their children and the state." [16] The way in which women can best benefit the state is to breast-feed their own children and thereby stop the "fearful slaughter each year . . . among these many thousands of unhappy nurslings." [17] In her study of the regulation of the wet-nursing business in eighteenth-century Hamburg, the social historian Mary Lindemann tells us that "physicians, philanthropists, and moralists alike" were exercised about the breast-feeding problem.[18] It should not be surprising then that the laws that Frank advocated became part of the Prussian legal code of 1794, in two articles under the section of the mutual rights and duties of parents and children. Article 67 read: "A healthy mother is required to breast-feed her child." Article 68 read: "It is, however, the father's right to decide on the length of time she shall give her breast to the child." [19]

In order to force mothers to conduct themselves for the benefit of the state, the reformers turned not only to law but also to the use of ideas, or what will be called ideological power. Lindemann aptly describes the two principal strategies employing ideological power to solve the problem of mothering. One strategy was to publicize the dangers of allowing children to associate with the corrupt women who were wet nurses while at the same time stressing that fathers were responsible for "good child-rearing practices" and through them for "the good of the state." [20] This is a bad woman, good father ideology, and as we will see, it was very much in harmony with traditional wisdom. The second strategy was to prize and praise "the salutary influence of the mother" and of natural femininity.[21] This is a good mother, feminine soul ideology and it was a new perception of women.

The poetic linkage between the good mother and the feminine soul was an innovation in two senses. First, it was a new wisdom or knowledge about women's natural feminine and maternal qualities and their beneficial effects on society. Second, it was a new punitive strategy aimed at the prevention of infanticide. Social reformers now sought to impress people and prevent crime with imaginary images, rather than with actual images of criminals being horribly torn apart and executed. This and other images were not only representations of real life, of what one reformer called representations of "the cruelties, abuses, vices and crimes, for the existence of which the prevailing religion, the severity or caprice and unnaturalness of many a law code is to blame." [22] They also increasingly became representations of ideal life, of what life ought to be. The poetic image of Gretchen was offered as an ideal. Through this strategy of disciplining women by imposing on them images of ideals, the images of the feminine soul took on an immense importance.

The Role of Ideology

The German social historian Karin Hausen points out that there is a relation between the new wisdom about women's unique qualities implicit in the feminine soul and the new disciplinary strategy. She contends that in the late eighteenth century a new way of defining the different gender characteristics of women and men was "discovered" in Germany. Before the end of the eighteenth century, definitions of women and men were based on their different statuses and duties in the feudal household, which formed the basis of the social structure of preindustrial Europe. In a 1735 encyclopedia, for example, *woman* is defined as "a married person, who subject to her husband's will and rule runs the household and in the latter is the servant's superior." [23] By the mid-nineteenth century in Germany, definitions of women were strikingly different. In a popular dictionary under the entry *woman,* we find: "[Woman] is more sympathetic, more moral, more religious than the rougher, often hard-hearted man who inclines to measure everything in terms of self." [24] In this short sentence we can see that woman is defined in terms of her uniquely religious soul and man in terms of a self, a marked "individuality," or what will be called in this history an autonomous ego. If we read further, we learn that woman's "virtue is . . . purity of heart." She is a "a more feeling creature" than man and he is a "more thinking creature" than woman. Woman's heightened emotionalism gives her a capacity for "inward participation and sympathy" that puts her in touch more readily than man with what is universal or eternal. And finally, we learn the Freudian truth that the normal woman's desire is the desire for a child: "It is woman's nature to love not her own sex, but rather the tender, helpless ones." [25]

In describing what is different in the eighteenth- and nineteenth-century definitions of man and woman, Hausen points out that "what is new . . . is the choice of referent." [26] The earlier definitions refer to a social status, what might be called an external place in a structured social order. The later ones refer to interior psychic qualities and their relation to social roles.

The "discovery" of women's uniquely feminine and maternal psychic qualities, lauded by Goethe and innumerable others, occurs just at the time of the "discovery" of man's autonomous ego. It occurs when men, in the name of their innate principle of freedom, are struggling in the late eighteenth century to reform feudal social, economic, and political structures. But they were trying to reform not only the external structure that oppressed them but also the women who were not cooperating in these efforts to form modern states and to ensure healthy populations. Thus in the new law codes, which were admired as models of reform, women were required by law to breast-feed their children. The goals of a healthy, strong state were thus imposed on women according to the manner of her perceived contribution.

Poetic representations in which women's unique spiritual qualities were praised were used to reinforce the values implicit in the law codes.

The new definitions of men and women and the new theories of crime and punishment followed by enlightened reformers and enlightened monarchs like Frederick who survived the revolutions represent more than a reaction against the excess of violence directed against the body of the criminal in the public spectacles of their torture and execution. According to Foucault in *Discipline and Punish,* the new theories sought to replace the body as the object of punishment with the soul of the criminal, which could become penitent and reformed in life and not merely at the point of a torturous death, as did Gretchen's in *Faust.*

What is of most importance for us is Foucault's claim that this humanitarian reform of horrible public physical punishment through concern for the soul of the criminal expanded the range and reach of punitive strategies.[27] In place of the body destroyed piece by piece by torture and death, humanitarian reformers sought to place a body rendered submissive through the control of ideas. Reformers sought ways to use the power of ideas to discipline bodies, and in doing so they tried to use the inner psyche, the mind or soul "as a surface of inscription for power," by presenting to it the images of proper human life in representations.[28]

Foucault quotes an advocate of this process of exercising power over the body through controlling ideas.

> When you have thus formed the chain of ideas in the heads of your citizens, you will then be able to pride yourselves on guiding them and being their masters. A stupid despot may constrain his slaves with iron chains; but a true politician binds them even more strongly with their own ideas; it is at the stable point of reason that he secures the end of the chain; this link is all the stronger in that we do not know of what it is made and we believe

it to be our own work; despair and time eat away the bonds of iron and steel, but they are powerless against the habitual union of ideas, they can only tighten it still more; and on the soft fibers of the brain is founded the unshakable base of the soundest of Empires.[29]

This is a striking description of the power that reformers thought they could gain by controlling ideas. The author asserts that a chain of ideas can be stronger and thus more effective in constraining people than a real chain of iron and steel. This chain is formed by what humans consider their own rational thought. By hanging certain ideas on the hook of that part of consciousness called reason, rulers and reformers can persuade people to believe that these are their own ideas. In fact, by hanging ideas from the hook of reason, people can be made to believe that these are *the* true ideas, that is, ideas that have a universal or even eternal truth. They can be made to believe "this is the way things are," and as apparently rational people they will live accordingly. Whereas people may come to rebel when actual iron chains weaken or, in other words, when the physical force of rulers is not strong enough to constrain them, they are powerless against the chain of ideas that has become habitual and accepted as their own.

Rulers and reformers did not consider the ideas they would impress "on the soft fibers of the brain" to be ideological in the sense of false or merely illusory. They too thought the ideas were true. They thought that with their minds freed from the false ideas of religious superstition they had been able to empirically study the real world. Through scientific investigation, they thought they had discovered the way things are. Thus, to implant these true ideas on the brains of the less enlightened would simultaneously constrain and liberate them!

This analysis of how reformers came to view their ability to change the behavior of other people underscores the importance of certain elements in the reasoning of European thinkers during this period. One important element in what is in effect a social science was the criticism of religion in the sense of dispelling superstition and belief in irrational forces. A second crucial element was the attempt of reformers to tie all ideas or representations to the "real" thing. In the physical sciences this may make sense. To tie mental representations of physical phenomena to the actual phenomena was, in fact, the aim of science. Today we can accept the effort, for example, to tie the representation of rain to quantitative definitions of air and water and to criticize a representation of it as a sign of a supernatural God's good pleasure. To implant scientific ideas about rain in the minds of farmers could help them develop better agricultural methods.

But what could it mean to tie mental representations of social life to the real thing? In Germany at this time, the real thing—actual social conditions—were unsatisfactory. Here German thinkers equated the real with the ideal, an equation made often by those called idealists. True social life, society as it can be lived by rational men, does not exist in the same way as do rain or stones or other physical phenomena. Yet rational men can develop, through reflection and their own rational scientific powers, the knowledge of what true human society should be. In this way German thinkers formulated a society as they thought it should be, and this knowledge was considered to be real, in the sense of scientific and true, and ideal, in the sense of not yet existing in real social conditions. The task of rational men committed to reforming society was to implant this true knowledge on the brains of less rational men— and on the brains of women.

When reformers turned to the practical matter of implanting their ideas, they concluded that poetic representations would be more effective than repetitions of their scientific modes of thought. Thus, to exercise their constraining and liberating ideological power, they called upon their poets to tell the people stories. Stories about the feminine soul thus arose in response to the new reliance on "ideological power" instead of brutal physical power to control the crime of infanticide and its extension in the problem of mothering.

The poets who imagined this feminine soul and the architects of this biopolitics assumed that *they* could control the ideology they had created. But this is not what happened. Although it was born in the context of biopolitics, the feminine soul at times took on a life of its own and threatened the success of this enlightened science of society. Sometimes, even in the discourses of men on their own moral development, this feminine soul resisted, indeed refused to refer solely to the interior of women's psyches, and began to refer to a female God. At that point, belief in the feminine soul ceased to serve as an ideological force to shape women for their place in the social order and flickered with the promise of subverting and transforming that order.

The Traditional Ideology

The German thinkers and reformers of the nineteenth century had assumed that they could control their new ideology because they already had in place a fully developed tradition of ideology and stories that had served their purposes of establishing and maintaining a certain social order. Handbooks for the conduct of the affairs of the feudal German household dominated German social structure into the eighteenth century. These handbooks, called housefather books, were the *Marriage Is Holy* books of German Protestantism. From the time of Luther on, Protestant religious leaders wrote manuals and pamphlets to spell out the God-given order of relationships and corresponding duties and virtues of members of the family within the household and within the broader society.

Liberal German men of the late eighteenth and early nineteenth centuries often related Luther's attribution of

religious meaning to marriage and his relocation of religious authority from the ecclesiastical hierarchy to the
family to their own challenges to political authority in
the name of their autonomy. Even Marx interpreted
Luther as a revolutionary who "shattered faith in authority." But Luther did this, according to Marx, only
"by restoring the authority of faith. He transformed the
priests into laymen by changing the laymen [i.e., house-
father] into priests." Nonetheless, "if Protestantism was
not the real solution [to the struggle for freedom] it at
least posed the problem correctly." [30] By that Marx
meant that the Lutheran shift of religious authority into
the home was a revolution in the dynamics of religion
that could be interpreted as a first tenous move toward
power to the people, that is, toward the affirmation of
political freedom and the struggle for participatory government. The most effective vehicle for bringing about
this shift of religious authority and turning laymen into
priests was the housefather books. What Marx and many
of the other historians fail to discuss is that these revolutionary books, written by religious men for fathers,
tell an old story about woman.

The housefather books, perhaps better than any
other premodern German literature, exemplify the definitions of man and woman that were prevalent prior
to the end of the eighteenth century. In them, woman is
defined in terms of her status in the household.[31] Furthermore, woman's status was based on the quality of
her religious soul as defined by the early religious reformers. In stark contrast to the soul she will receive in
the nineteenth century, this one is a religiously defective one that legitimates her subservience to her husband's rule.

In the housefather books, man is also defined in
terms of his status in the household. He is, of course,
the married person who rules and subjects the woman
to his will. Julius Hoffmann, the author of the definitive
study of housefather books, explains that the term *father,*

which is the one most used to describe the man, refers directly to a power relation and not, as in our contemporary usages, to a biological component in reproduction or even to a role in parenting.[32] It takes no subtle sociological analysis to see that the power relation equated with the father in these books is the same as the power relation equated with God the father. The books plainly say so.

These marriage manuals prescribe that God the father's relation to humans be replicated in the father's relation to woman and in all other relations in the household. All sets of relationships, husband and wife, parent and child, household owner and peasant, are to be modeled on the inequality of God and man in the economy of salvation.[33] The fundamental pattern of power relation is this: God is to man as man is to woman (and as all superiors are to subordinates in the house). Asymmetry in sex, age, and social level characterized the Christian order of the household.

The linchpin of this order was the father's religious soul. On his right relationship to God, which he was to achieve by cultivating the virtue of fear of the Lord, rested the entire order of the household. Complementing his fear of the Lord was the father's rationality by which he controlled his desires and emotions.[34] The strength and authority of the father's religious soul, secured by fearing God above and controlling the passions below, was the source of all order in the household. As might be expected, the virtue of trust in God fades behind the fear of God in these books.[35]

The Book of Genesis reveals that the power arrangement in the household is of divine origin. From this book, housefathers learn that the deed of Eve in eating the apple proves that woman "was not obedient to God and could not control herself." As a consequence, God rendered her subordinate to man and gave him the authority and duty to control her.[36] So it is woman's defective soul that necessitates her subordination to the rule of her husband and gives him his pride of place in this social order.[37] Without the saving soul of her husband, say these marriage books, woman is "incapable of a full religious and moral life." [38]

It follows as the night the day that where Eve's primal disobedience defines woman, obedience is lauded as her primary virtue. And with the exception of the father's virtue of fear of God, obedience is the household virtue to which these books gave the most attention. Obviously, the wife's disobedience could seriously threaten the divinely ordained order of the household. When a countermodel to Eve is offered to women for emulation, it is most often Sarah, the incredibly patient and obedient wife of the patriarch Abraham. Protestant housefather authors, like Luther himself, were leery of the more customary countermodel, the Virgin Mary, because in the medieval Catholicism against which they rebelled she tended to disengage herself from her inverse earthly image and take on divine powers of her own.

At the root of Eve's disobedience lay an even deeper vice, the allure and seductive sexual desire of her body. Because of this vice, for the wife even the virtue of love had to be obedience. Housefather authors commonly attributed Adam's sin of eating the apple to his sexual passion for Eve.[39] Luther warned against that "intoxicating" love which can invade early marriage and blind man.[40] Strong sexual attraction was considered an outright danger in marriage because it threatened man's rational control of his desires and, even more, as it did with Adam, his most important virtue—fear of the Lord. And, as the story goes, this was woman's fault, a fault she carried around all the time in her body.

Hoffmann explains that for the housefather married love meant agape, not eros. It meant a mutual sympathy and willingness to sacrifice the self for the other, which was rooted in God's willingness to sacrifice his son for humanity. Moreover, in marriage this mutuality is interpreted as completely congruent with the asymmetry

2. *Biopolitics and the Birth of the Feminine Soul*   47

of the power relation between God the father and humans. According to Hoffmann, the unity of wills that was to be achieved by mutual sympathy was not at all like the erotic ideal of loss of self in another but represented the proper ordering of wills.[41] In this view, marital love is based on hierarchical submission of wills, the wife's to the husband's and the husband's to God. Housefather authors described the achievement of married love as a husbandly art similar to that of sailing a ship; the artful sailor knows how to exert just the right amount of control for smooth sailing.[42] In exercising this art, husbands love their wives like God loves humans, tolerating and being patient with their weaknesses up to the point of disobedience. But when a wife disobeys, a housefather should "have a man's heart in his body" and discipline his wife with physical force if necessary.[43] It is clear enough that the rule of the husband's God-fearing soul was the source of marital love and that woman's desire had to conform completely to her obedience to it—or else.

Prescriptions in housefather books governing the conduct of women reflect a deep fear of the power of female sexual desire. The rash of witch burnings in the sixteenth and seventeenth centuries, when housefather books first became popular, is another reflection of this fear. Both reflections were images of the same perception of women and prompted the authors of housefather books to identify women who went to extremes to suppress their desire as the most exemplary housemothers. According to Steven Ozment, one of the most popular housefather books "found especially inspiring the reported custom in contemporary India of the most favored wife's joining her deceased husband on his funeral pyre." [44] Ozment speculates that such depictions of "heroic wives may reflect . . . the traditional view of woman as temptresses." [45] No doubt. It is hard to miss the logic of this view: A good woman's willingness to be burned and the burning of bad women as witches not only reflected but were systemically derived from the perception of women as the temptress Eve. The purpose of the Hindu practice of suttee was to protect the honor of widows and thus of their dead husbands. It was better for these women to burn than to give in, as it was presumed they would, to a seducer.[46] Like Eve, they were cursed by a weakness of will and an excess of sexual desire, and to control the latter they willingly followed their husbands to death.[47] Thus for the housefathers suttee was the symbol of the good woman's suppression of desire.

Finally, it is important to note what by now should be obvious. The father must be the parent responsible for the religious and moral development of the child. It is true, as Ozment stresses, that in relation to the young child mothers are given a place of authority and rule at the side of fathers. Nevertheless, "the authors of the housefather books, fearing that mothers would always be too soft, too filled with blind, indulgent love for their children to administer a regular discipline, insisted that fathers should take the dominant role in child rearing after the age of six or seven." [48] Further, mothers could assume an "equal" role even in early childhood education only by virtue of their obedience to and conformity with the will of their husbands. Neither maternal instincts nor female desire had any positive value for these authors.[49]

In the context of the world defined by the housefather books, the religious value of women was tenuous at best. A weak-willed creature with a defective soul, woman had a character that could become truly moral only when subjected to her husband's will and guidance. With full control over this old ideology of woman, modern reformers expected to be able to control a new one that would serve new purposes. Ultimately, they succeeded, but not before dangerous representations of the feminine soul were created.

3

The Feminine Soul in Leonard and Gertrude

[Gertrude] alone seemed to possess a soul untainted by the moral filth around her.[1]

PESTALOZZI, *Leonard and Gertrude*

As individuals express their life, so they are. What they are, therefore, coincides with what they produce, with what *they produce and* how *they produce. The nature of individuals thus depends on the material conditions which determine their production.*[2]

MARX, *The German Ideology*

The production of people is . . . qualitatively different from the production of things.[3]

ROSE, *"Hand, Brain, and Heart: A Feminist Epistemology for the Natural Sciences."*

LEONARD AND GERTRUDE was a widely read novel about ideal family and social life. Like the housefather books, it was read for the edification and instruction of husbands, wives, and children, but in this late eighteenth-century text, the wife's soul is, beyond all doubt, religiously superior to her husband's. The author of the text, Johann Friedrich Pestalozzi, broke with generations of Protestant household wisdom over the crime of infanticide.

Pestalozzi was among those late eighteenth-century men who believed that infanticide was the most serious crime of the day. He wrote *Leonard and Gertrude* while he was preparing in 1780 to enter a literary contest on the topic "What are the best and most practicable means to eradicate infanticide without promoting prostitution?" [4] The drama of the editorial announcing this contest reminds us of the degree of concern about infanticide that was felt by state officials and moral reformers at that time in Germany.

> There are crimes committed among us which are the most horrible and at the same time the most common, and among these is infanticide; crimes which are related to virtues, virtues which develop into vices, and among these too is infanticide; crimes which experience teaches are not made less frequent by increasing the severity of the punishment, while not to punish them would bring disgrace to mankind and destruction to law and order, and among these too is infanticide.... How long shall we lead to the block these unfortunate girls as sacrificial victims, whose love and the natural weakness of their sex, whose adornment of innocence and modesty has made them to be mothers and murderesses? [5]

As it turned out, Pestalozzi did not enter the contest —because he felt he had too much to say, not too little. As his biographer says, he assiduously examined "the connections between circumstances and crime, crime and punishment, punishment and education, education and national tradition, national tradition and morals."[6] He concluded that, to a large degree, crime could be prevented by improving morals and that morals could be improved by representations.[7] He added that the best means of reform was to produce good hearts in people, not to put them in chains.

This conclusion by itself would make Pestalozzi's work memorable, but he went even further. Along with many of his contemporaries, Pestalozzi sought to prevent infanticide both as physical and as spiritual murder of children by representing a woman's moral and religious superiority, but his representation got out of hand and the feminine soul he depicted took on a life of its own. Although his pedagogical theories were adopted by progressive German leaders as a model for the kind of education that could form citizens for a strong and modern German fatherland, Pestalozzi's own continued fascination with the cultural and religious potential of his heroine's soul drew criticism and cautions from his admirers and charges of heresy from his detractors. Despite the number and strength of his critics, the story remained popular well into the nineteenth century. We will examine the criticisms against his strategy for the prevention of infanticide through the ideology of the good mother after we review the story of *Leonard and Gertrude.*

The Narrative of Leonard and Gertrude

Leonard and Gertrude is set in the late feudal Protestant village of Bonnal, which was ruled by the good and enlightened "father of the people," the lord Arner.[8] His bailiff Hummel, the mediator of justice between the father of the people and his sons, is the villain. Leonard is the village mason and Gertrude is his wife. Leonard and many of the poor men in the village are in debt to

the wicked bailiff, who threatens them with imprisonment if they do not spend their meager wages in the
tavern he owns. Through his position, he forces the poor
men into drunkenness and keeps their families in dire
poverty and misery.

The action of the novel begins when Gertrude visits
Arner to seek his help in extricating Leonard from
Hummel's evil clutches. Arner listens to her complaints
and promises to help her. He arranges to build a new
church in the village in order to give Leonard, the mason, and other poor men more lucrative work. The lord
also informs Hummel that tavern keeping and the duties
of public office can no longer be combined and he orders him to choose which job he wants to keep.

Hummel is infuriated by Arner's intervention into
the affairs of the village. As a result, he plots to sabotage
the building of the church, to discredit Leonard and
Gertrude, and to encourage the peasants to rob the lord.
Meanwhile, in the house of Leonard and Gertrude, peace
and harmony have been restored. In fact, Gertrude begins to spread this family peace to her neighbors, beginning next door at the home of a poor widower named
Hubel-Rudy. She takes over the care of the children
and sets about finding him a wife.

As Hummel's attempts at sabotaging the reform of
the village fail one by one, he hits upon a final desperate
plan: He will go into the forest at night and move the
boundary stone of Arner's land, thereby causing the
lord to lose a large portion of of it. But when he goes to
the forest, he is frightened by what he thinks is the devil
and he runs back to the village to confess all his crimes.
The wicked bailiff is then brought before the lord for
punishment.

With the power of the bailiff finally broken, Arner
makes additional attempts to reform Bonnal. But these
are met with resistance and intrigue on the part of
the landowners and the more well-to-do peasants. Finally, with the help of Gertrude, he discovers an effective

means of reform—education. He opens a school, under the direction of his former minister for economic affairs, Gluelphi, modeled on how Gertrude teaches her children in her own home. He also sees that land is divided among the poorer peasants, debts are paid, and stolen property returned to its rightful owner. When it looks like justice will finally be restored in Bonnal, the peace of the village is threatened one last time by Arner's jealous and greedy cousin Sylvia, who plots to discredit his management in the eyes of their uncle, the duke. Her plot fails and, in the end, the duke is convinced that Arner's principles of reform can be applied to the government of the country as a whole.

This is the basic plot of the story, and in its bare outline there is a sense in which *Leonard and Gertrude* can be called a housefather book. It is a narrative representation of the successful attempts of the father of the people to restore order and justice in his extended household, his realm. Like the housefather books, this is a tale about the father's kingdom and his rightly ordered relationship to his sons. Disorder is the disease that runs through the society of Bonnal—religious disease in the disorder of superstitious madness, moral disease in the disorder of the passions, and, most fundamentally, domestic disease in the disorder of the relationships between husbands and wives, parents and children.

But this is a housefather book with a twist. Domestic disease is primarily represented in terms of men's flawed relationships with wives and children, whom they neglect and beat. This is certainly a housefather society gone awry and the rule of the lord is ineffectual by itself in restoring order. In Pestalozzi's version of the housefather book, it is the innately good mother, Gertrude, who shows the father the way. It is in the soul of Gertrude that the lord finds the social medicine capable of establishing order in his realm. Let us look now at the changes introduced by Pestalozzi into the traditional housefather book.

THE FATHER'S FEAR OF THE LORD

The story begins with Leonard returning home from one of his bouts at the tavern to find Gertrude and his seven children desperately sobbing about their poverty. This scene represents an incident that has been repeated over and over again in every village home in which the father does not have a good relationship with the lord. In this instance, sobered by the sight of his family's sorrow, Leonard confesses to Gertrude for the first time that Hummel's threat of imprisonment for his unpaid debts is the reason for his sojourns to Hummel's tavern. In a direct reversal of the plot of housefather books, Leonard reveals himself to be crippled, rather than strengthened, by his fear of the lord. He is afraid of going to Arner with his problem. By clear contrast, Gertrude has the courage to do so, and she takes off, babe in arms, to face the lord. Thus she initiates the lord's attempts to restore justice in Bonnal.

Arner's initial response to the evils and injustice in his realm is, significantly, a material one. He gives Gertrude money immediately and, as we saw, plans to give work to Leonard and ten of the poorest men of the village by having them build a church. Only afterward does Arner begin his long series of attempts to bring about spiritual or moral reform.

Arner's first efforts at reform are directed at Hummel, with whom he takes a number of enlightened steps. By demanding that Hummel choose between the position of bailiff and the village tavern, Arner, in effect, psychologically tortures Hummel until he eventually confesses his crimes. Driven mad with resentment against Arner for destroying the conditions for his criminal activity and by his own unsuccessful methods for restoring them, Hummel tries with one definitive act to destroy the lord's realm by moving a boundary stone. While struggling in the dark forest with the heavy stone, he is terrorized by a monstrous creature who howls, "Hummel, you are mine!" [9] We, the readers, know all along what

Hummel does not: The "devil" is Arner's poulterer, who accidentally came on Hummel and decided to frighten him to prevent his moving the boundary stone. But the superstitious Hummel is certain he is the devil come to steal his soul, and he runs from the forest in abject fear to immediately tell all his crimes to the pastor.

To force Hummel to lose his self-control was important to Arner's plan for reforming Bonnal. The maddened bailiff displays irrationality and superstitious religious belief. Like other enlightened reformers, Arner was convinced that the exorcism of irrationality and superstition from the minds and souls of the people was an essential element in their liberation from vice and criminal behavior. He is convinced that to reform the people, he must make them see this criminal irrationality and superstition.

PUNISHMENT BY REPRESENTATION

As lord of the realm, Arner must punish Hummel. He begins his punishment by articulating the traditional theory of punishment of his time, the one that prescribed live burial, impalement, and tortured drowning for infanticides. He exclaims to Hummel, "Unhappy man! It grieves me to the heart to inflict upon you, in your old age, the punishment which necessarily follows misdeeds like yours. You have deserved death, not because Rudy's meadow [which he had stolen] or my boundary stone are worth a man's life, but because a career of perjury and robbery can bring an unlimited amount of danger and suffering upon a whole community." [10] Like the lawmakers of the same period, who looked at the prevalence of the crime rather than its seriousness, Arner looked at the extent of Hummel's crimes rather than the nature of them and asserted that this criminal's "deserved" punishment must match the breadth of social effect of his acts. But Arner also mitigates the deserved punishment on humanitarian grounds—Hummel's advanced age.

In place of sending the criminal to a real death, Arner condemns Hummel to go through an imaginary death at a mock execution, explaining that a public representation of death is necessary as an example in a society in which "there are so many rude and unprincipled people." [11] At the mock execution, the hangman cries to Hummel, "Thou hast deserved that thy bones should rot here, and the birds of heaven feed upon thy flesh!" [12]

Hummel's punishment also involves a second type of representation for the sake of the unprincipled people. Arner commands him to talk to the pastor everyday for two weeks and to give him a "history of your life, with your domestic troubles, your hard-heartedness, your contempt of oaths, and your injustice to the poor and rich alike; and this must be confirmed by your own testimony." [13] The purpose of this two-week talk was not merely to provide therapy of soul for Hummel, but to give the pastor narrative material for his own contribution to the reform and discipline of the people. In a sermon, the pastor retold this history of the criminal's life and the story went straight "to the hearts of all his congregation; it seemed as if the Bailiff were a mirror in the pastor's hands, from which each one of the multitude saw his own sins reflected." [14] But even this mirroring of sinful souls along with the representation of death at the gallows fails to bring order and justice to Bonnal.

Greedy overseers corrupt Hummel's successor as bailiff, Meyer, who waffles in his loyalty to Arner and allows theft. Moreover, the overseers "disseminated" superstitious nonsense encouraging the belief in ghosts and witches. So once again Arner must resort to representational tactics to reform Bonnal. He stages a dramatic reenactment of the devil drama in the forest in which the true human identity of the devil is revealed in order to make the people see the foolishness of their superstition. He then holds a collective trial at which he displays the actual crimes of the powerful overseers and the poor peasants alike. Significantly, he tries to join material and spiritual reforms by providing more land along with trees and animals to the peasants at this spectacle. But to no avail. Happy with their new life free of the corrupt overseers, the peasants return to lives of uncontrolled passion.

None of Arner's representational tactics succeeds. Despite his efforts to clear away irrationality and superstition, Arner cannot find that hook, that "stable point of reason," upon which to hang the ideas that he believes will both constrain and liberate his people.[15] That is, not until he takes a closer look at Gertrude.

GERTRUDE'S UNTAINTED SOUL

When Arner looks closely at Gertrude, he discovers that "the only cottage in the village which was free from the turbulent unrest of this period was that of Gertrude. She alone seemed to possess a soul untainted by the moral filth around her." [16] Like the reader, Arner wonders what characterizes this salvific soul of Gertrude. He learns that she has inscribed certain rules in her soul and lives according to them.[17] It is worth reading a number of these.

Be silent about everything which does not concern you.
Do not speak of that which you do not understand.
Step aside when people speak either too loud or too softly.
Learn well what it is necessary for you to use.
Let your head and heart always be in the right place, and
        never in many at once, but always with you.
Serve with body and soul those to whom you are in-
        debted, and those you love.[18]

Because these sayings were inscribed in her soul, Gertrude "had attained to a remarkable degree of domestic and social wisdom, and throughout the confusion which reigned in the village, no word escaped her lips which could give rise to misunderstandings, not a syllable which could provide either enmity or ridicule." [19]

Gertrude's soul, then, is permeated by order, stocked full of measure. Without a doubt, her soul is a stable point of reason—the perfect hook for a reformer's disciplining chain of ideas. Uttering no word that could "give rise to misunderstandings," Gertrude is in fact a domestic scientist. Like a scientist, she ties the elemental representations of words to the way things are. Hers is a plain, lucid speech. Thus from the order innate in her soul emanate the principles of that science of society upon which reformers sought to found a new social order. And, indeed, her soul becomes the source of order and discipline in Bonnal.

Within her own home, Gertrude orders everything—physical space, time, religious practice, her children's moral lives, and their learning. Granted, she did step out of her home to order the affairs of her husband, and in taking this step, Gertrude seems to have gone too far. Her salvific soul is only discovered by the lord after she returns home and resumes a normal life.

At first, the secret of her soul is revealed only to her next-door neighbor, the widower Hubel-Rudy. Visiting Hubel-Rudy's home after the death of his mother, which followed the death of his wife by three months, Gertrude finds it in total disorder. She informs Hubel-Rudy that this disorder "is a deep-rooted disease, which you must set to work in earnest to cure." [20] She guides him in this task by first putting his house and children in order. She teaches his children, as she does her own, to be attentive to the physical care of their bodies and to observe the condition of things around them. So that they can learn to be productive workers, she teaches them to spin and sew. And what is most remarkable, during their spinning and sewing, "she taught them to count and cipher, for she regarded arithmetic as the foundation of all intellectual order." [21] Wonderfully, this domestic scientist had no math anxiety. On the contrary, she takes it upon herself to train children in scientific method and observation.

Gertrude's next job is to find Hubel-Rudy a good

wife, but before doing so, she must train him to recognize one. Explaining to him that his former wife sowed seeds of disorder in his home, she declares that the woman did not even know how "to do for her husband and children what costs nothing" [22]—providing a clean living space, attending to children even in "trifles," making sure that they "not be left to themselves all day." [23]

Before long, Arner will come to appreciate these free, society-saving services of the good wife. It is when he learns how to integrate their material value into his program for reform that he discovers how to manage the government of Bonnal. Nonetheless, even though these services of the good mother come to figure in the economy of Bonnal, their physical cost to the body of a woman, a cost the body of Hubel-Rudy's wife could not pay, does not. Gertrude discounts this physical cost to the female body in the name of the strength of her soul. Hubel-Rudy objects to her harsh words about his wife and tells Gertrude that he felt sympathy toward her because for "all her slovenliness, she was always so pious, and made the children say their prayers." [24] Gertrude responds, "Ah, there can be no true piety without energy, and when one is slovenly, one can neither pray properly one's self, nor teach it to one's children." [25] In Gertude's view, untainted souls generate a boundless, cost-free, physical energy.

The apparent religiosity of the neighbor's wife is carefully reduced to a meaningless escape. Instead of confronting her family's poverty and hunger with an energy of body, Hubel-Rudy's wife became depressed and took to her bed, where she read books that filled her mind with dreams and visions. A product of a disorderly home herself, this depressed mother had fallen at an early age "into the hands of the Parson Flieg, who filled her head with dreams and speculations about the revelation [of the Apocalypse] of St. John." [26] Even when she had a home and children, she acted as if she had nothing in the world to do but read about these mythical visions. Hubel-Rudy exclaims, "Yes, I was sometimes afraid she would set the house on fire, she was so absent-minded over her books. They were her sanctuary and her heaven, so that she forgot me and the children and everything else." [27]

Notice the contrast between what went on in the mind of this woman and what characterizes the soul of Gertrude. The former's mind was filled with dreams and visions, and the latter's soul is inscribed with both reality and duty. On Gertrude's soul is written such rules as "Let your head and heart always be in the right place, and never in many at once, but always with you" and "Serve with body and soul those to whom you are indebted, and those you love." [28] Devoid of these rules, the soul of Hubel-Rudy's wife was that of a woman who might accidentally burn down her home and thereby kill her children; she was a potential infanticide. Her visionary reading destroyed her own constitution, and only her death, not her dreams, saved the life of her children.

The only other depiction of a bad woman in this story also calls to mind infanticide. The other woman is Sylvia, the cousin of the lord, Arner, and she too had been corrupted by the reading of books. In her case, the education available to aristocratic women served merely to conceal her devious and scheming character. When the people discover that Sylvia is undermining Arner's reforms in the hope of discrediting him and receiving his property from their uncle, the duke, they take her punishment in their own hands. While she is journeying alone from the castle to the village, one of the villagers allows his dog to attack her. The dog viciously claws at her and rips off the bodice of her gown in a mock tearing of the flesh, representing the real tearing of flesh with glowing tongs that was part of the standard punishment for infanticide.

Gertrude ends her instruction of Hubel-Rudy by explaining to him that poor mothers produce daughters who in turn become poor mothers. If mothers do not provide their daughters with rules that enable them to "know, from the time they get up in the morning till they go to bed at night, just what they have to do . . . the most docile and happy-hearted girl, when she grows up and has children of her own, may become so despondent and unlike herself that no one would recognize her." [29] She will grow up, as did his wife, to be a potential infanticide.

Hubel-Rudy learns his lesson. He exclaims, "It would be like being in heaven" to have a good wife with a soul like Gertrude's.[30]

SECRETS OF REFORM

The saving qualities of Gertrude's soul are extended to the whole village when Arner brings his minister for economic affairs, Gluelphi, to learn how she raises her children in her own home. It is then that Arner discovers that by integrating the material value of the society-saving services of the good wife into his program for reform, he can at last reform the morals of the people. His economic minister learns from watching Gertrude teach her children that "the proper education of the youthful population [is] the only means of elevating the condition of the corrupt village." [31] Inspired by her method of teaching, Gluelphi gives up his job in economic management to open a school.

Ruler and reformer thus discover the way to enable the people to root out evil from their souls.[32] They have found "the stable point of reason" upon which to hang a chain of true ideas that the villagers will accept as their own. With Gertrude's help, Gluelphi comes to know the village children "in eight days better than their parents did in eight years," [33] and he uses this knowledge "to keep their hearts open before his eyes." [34] With his constant attention to every moment and detail of the children's lives, Gluelphi, like Gertrude, is in complete control of what enters their hearts and minds. Now he, the agent of the government of the lord, can "teach them to see and hear with accuracy." [35] He can impress the souls of the villagers with the ideas he wants them to hold, knowing that the villagers will accept these ideas as true and live by them.

The pastor also takes instruction from Gertrude. It is important to realize that the pastor is, like the lord, an enlightened man. In contrast to Parson Flieg, who misled Hubel-Rudy's wife through books, the village pastor does not teach women—or men—about the cosmic drama of salvation portrayed in the Revelation of Saint John, since the mythic quality encourages dreams and visions. In fact, he had cooperated with Arner in demonstrating to the villagers that belief in the devil was superstitious. Thus, this religious leader did not believe in the literal truth of the biblical representations. Clearly he thought that without the guidance of reason, these were open to misinterpretation. Yet he had been confident that theological words were reliable, that instructing children in doctrinal differences between Christian confessions and making them memorize long prayers were safe and effective methods of religious education. But Gertrude teaches him a new method.

After seeing the success of her home training, the pastor is convinced that "verbal instruction, in so far as it aims at true human wisdom, and at the highest goal of this wisdom, true religion, ought to be subordinated to a constant training in practical domestic labor." [36] He comes to see that "a quiet industrious life" (like that Gertrude creates in her home with her strength of soul) is the basis of "the foundations of a silent worship of God and love of humanity." [37] In order to replicate the effect of her soul in his own work, he develops a new theological science, tying religious representations to things as they are. "He connected every word of his brief religious teachings with [the children's] actual, every-day experience, so that when he spoke of God and eternity, it seemed to them as if he were speaking of father and mother, house and home, in short, of the things with which they were most familiar." [38]

Acknowledging the debt of the village to Gertrude,

Gluelphi tells her, "There can be no substitute for your mother's heart, which I must have for my school." [39] Gertrude demures and responds, "My mother's heart is hardly large enough for my own room, and if you are really to be our schoolmaster, I know you will bring a father's heart and a father's strength into the work, such as will make my little mother's heart quite superfluous." [40] From this exchange emerges a premise of moral reform—the cooperation of a mother's heart is a necessary complement to a father's heart.

Does all of this drama merely serve as a repetition of what every housefather book from Luther's time on prescribed—the cooperation of a mother's heart is a necessary complement to a father's heart? Not quite. In this version of the story of the father's establishment of his kingdom, woman and traditional religion are displaced. Despite Gertrude's humility with Gluelphi, in the salvation of Bonnal her soul has taken a place above the rule of her husband, Leonard, and the rule of all other men in Bonnal, including that of the lord and the pastor. The wisdom of her soul even displaces biblical representations of the kingdom of God and theological creeds. But this should hardly have been threatening, because her soul *is* the order of the father's kingdom itself. It is still the soul of the good housewife, a soul of domestic order, which in turn is the soul of the entire social order. Gertrude's soul is both the symbol and source of harmonious social relations between husband and wife, parent and child, and the lord and his people.

4

Divinization and Suppression
of Gertrude's Soul

*Women soon come into opposition to civilization
and display their retarding and restraining influence
—those very women who, in the beginning, laid
the foundation of civilization by the claims
of their love.*[1]

FREUD, *Civilization and Its Discontents*

*To admit the truth of the women's perspective to
the concept of moral development is to recognize
for both sexes the importance throughout life of
the connection between self and other, the
universality of the need for compassion
and care.*[2]

CAROL GILLIGAN, *In a Different Voice*

*[Love] is directed as a rule far more strongly and
decisively towards the sterner parent, the father,
who is more often absent, and who does not appear
directly as a benefactor, than towards the mother,
who with her beneficence is ever present.*[3]

JOHANN FICHTE, *Addresses to the German Nation*

As my mother leaves *her healthy children and*
clings *to the sickly, and* takes double care *of the*
wretched because she must, being the mother,
because she stands in God's place to the child,
so must I, if the mother is in God's place *to me,*
and God fills my heart in the mother's place.

*A feeling like the mother's feeling impels me. Man
is my brother, my love embraces the whole
race. . . . I am a child of God; I believed in my
mother, her heart showed me God. God is the
God of my* mother, *of* my heart *and* her heart.
I know no other God.[4]

PESTALOZZI, *How Gertrude Teaches Her Children*

THE REPRESENTATION OF GERTRUDE'S untainted soul appeared threatening to men. Why? One is tempted to answer that *any* change in the status of women's bodies or souls must be a threat to the economy of the father's rule. But this is too simple because it does not take into account that Gertrude's soul is a representation that was created as a tool of ideological power, as a means of producing women with good souls. The representation of Gertrude's soul should have been perceived as the image that those reformers like Johann Peter Frank, the theoretician of a medical police, were seeking in their efforts to exercise ideological power. What could be more effective, as Frank put it, to "force" the practice of proper mothering and eliminate infanticide? Would not this representation of the superior feminine soul of woman, in which Gertrude's soul is subordinated in the end to a great father's masculine soul and rule, force women to give and to give what "costs nothing"—their boundless physical energy—for the benefit of the state?

As we explore the answers to these questions, we shall discover that the religious quality of Gertrude's soul was central to its potential as a threat to the reformers' illusions that they could control ideological power. The representation of the religious quality of the feminine soul escapes the control of men and leads, on the one hand, to a female God and, on the other, to the female body.

First we will look at why religious leaders found its religious quality threatening. Then we will look at how Pestalozzi defended that quality by intensifying it. And finally, we will look at the suppression of that quality in the official appropriation of Pestalozzi's theory of education by the German philosopher and state official Johann Fichte, who rejected the religious meaning of the feminine soul in favor of the autonomous ego of man.

The Response of Christian Ministers

In *Leonard and Gertrude,* Christian ministers read about the superiority of a woman's religious wisdom to that of a minister, the pastor of Bonnal, and they responded according to the beliefs of their time, according to both religious and ideological beliefs. Although Pestalozzi and the Christian ministers recognized that the representation of Gertrude's soul was an ideal in the sense of a product of the mind or imagination, they and other proponents of ideological power also thought ideals were true. Readers understood that Pestalozzi's representation of an untainted feminine soul producing good mothers was expected to be accepted as real in that it represented the way things *could* be but are not. Further, Pestalozzi expected his representation to be accepted as real in that it represented the way in which some mothers actually nurture their children. Finally, although like Gluelphi in his story, Pestalozzi opened schools for the poor children of villages, he also promoted home education. He genuinely believed in an innate quality of women that enabled some women, including poor women, to be Gertrudes. His novel *Leonard and Gertrude* was testimony to his belief that this innate quality could be evoked by representation and thereby enable all women, poor and rich alike, to become Gertrudes.

Pestalozzi's contemporaries in the church could not accept the reality of Gertrude's feminine soul. He complained that ever since he began to express his hopes for social reform through mothers, "men cry out at me from all sides, 'The mothers of this country will never do it.' " [5] The most vehement of those men were Christian ministers, whose job was to "teach the people Christianity." They scorned him and said, "You may run up and down our villages, you will find no mothers who will do what you ask of them." [6] These Christian male critics of Pestalozzi had not encountered any real Gertrudes, and could not imagine any. Perhaps they could not imagine what mothers did with their children until they were six or seven.

Pestalozzi admitted that under the given social and economic conditions most mothers were not Gertrudes, but he placed the blame for this less on the conditions of poverty in villages like Bonnal than on the influence of Christian ministers on mothers. In doing so, he criticized the social effects of Christianity with an intensity worthy of Marx. But he departed from other critics in the focus of his criticism. He criticized ministers, not because they presented religious representations to the people, but because they refused to present the correct religious representations.

Pestalozzi responded to the religious despisers of mothers, "I would answer the men who dare to say 'run up and down the country, *the mothers of the land* will not do it or wish to do it,' and say, 'You ought to cry out to these unnatural mothers of our fatherland as Christ once cried to Jerusalem, 'Mothers! mothers! we would have gathered you together under the wings of wisdom, humanity, and Christianity, as a hen gathereth her chickens, *But ye would not.*' " [7]

In citing the Bible against his male critics, Pestalozzi chose one of the few passages in which God is imaged as a female, indeed, as a mother hen. If Christian preachers would dare to present this representation of God as female to mothers and if it then proved to have no social effect, he declared, "I will be silent and believe in their word and in their experience—and not in the mothers of the land, not in the heart that God has put into their breast. But if they dare not do this, I will not believe in them, but in the mothers of the land, and in the heart that God has put in their breast." [8]

Pestalozzi related the failure of Christian preachers to present this biblical representation of the divine maternity to their fundamental disregard of and disrespect for the poor. This failure, he claimed, is equivalent to throwing "away the people of the land as if they were the produce of a lower order of creation." [9] He reflected, "Throughout my whole life, I have seen and known all kinds of such wordy men wrapped up in systems and theories, *knowing nothing and caring nothing for the people;* and the individuals, who today slander the people in this way about this matter of education are more in this state than any others that I know. Such men think themselves upon a height, and the people far below them in the valley." [10]

Disbelief in the religious quality of the souls of mothers, of the heart God has put in their breasts, and disbelief in the divine maternity itself stems from Christian theologians' own oppressive delusions of grandeur. "The brilliant polish, which these wordy men owe to the unnatural way of living, makes them incapable of understanding that they are mounted on stilts, and therefore *must come down from their miserable wooden legs,* in order to stand as firmly as other folk, upon God's earth. I pity them. I have heard many of these wretched wordy men say, with a mixture of nun-like innocence and rabbinical wisdom: 'What can be more beautiful for the people than the Heidelberg Catechism and the Psalter'?" [11] The Heidelberg Catechism was the basic Lutheran catechism and it, along with the Book of Psalms, were the standard pedagogical tools of housefathers in the religious instruction of their children after the ages of six and seven.

In defense of the superiority of the religious quality of Gertrude's soul as a pedagogical text, Pestalozzi located the fundamental flaw of wordiness in males, a flaw that is at the root of the theologians' insistence on the priority of Christian doctrine in religious education and that consistently led them into false action. He wrote, "Yes, friend! I will excuse them this error of the human mind, it has always been and will be ever so. Men are all alike, the scribes and their disciples were so too. Then I will not open my mouth again against the verbosity of their social dogmas, against the tinkling cymbals of the ceremonies, and the loveless and foolish frame of mind that they must, by their very nature, produce; but, with the greatest man who ever declared the cause of truth, of the people and of love victorious against the errors of the scribes, I will only say, *'Father, forgive them; for they know not what they do.'* " [12]

To the Christian ministers about whom he was speaking, this charge had to imply the most heretical of reversals of Christian truth: Men not women are the source of original sin. Aside from Jesus, whom Pestalozzi interpreted as a liberator of the poor, men and not women, not Eve, have an intrinsic flaw in their minds or souls. This flaw manifests itself in males' oppressive use of words, in a verbosity that reproduces their loveless and foolish frames of mind. In effect, Pestalozzi held that men need mothers with souls like that of Gertrude to save them from the distortion innate in their souls.

Pestalozzi criticized traditional Christianity as a *male* ideology serving to oppress both women and the people, indeed, all people through its denigration of women. The theologians' type of religion is the opiate of the people. Clearly, in his criticism of this type of religion, he rivaled Marx. But unlike Marx, Pestalozzi did not equate religion itself with the opiate of the people. He believed in another type of religion, that of the mother.

THE THREAT OF WOMEN'S RELIGIOUS AUTONOMY TO PROGRESSIVES

Pestalozzi's conception of Gertrude's soul was perceived as a threat by Christian ministers in part because it could not simply be dismissed as groundless. *Leonard and Gertrude* fit squarely in the German Protestant tradition and threatened the perceptions of reformers from within that tradition. The same was true for progressive, political philosophers and their tradition. Like the housefather books, *Leonard and Gertrude* transferred religious authority from the religious leaders outside the family to the soul of a parent inside the family. Marx and many of his contemporaries recognized in Luther's affirmation of the religious autonomy of housefathers the beginning of the development of political autonomy. In transferring religious authority to a parent in the family, *Leonard and Gertrude* conformed to the progressive German political tradition, but in transferring it to the mother, Pestalozzi defied that tradition.

This transfer of religious authority to the souls of mothers implied a different political dynamic than that which Marx and historians found in Luther's transfer of religious authority to the souls of fathers. In contrast to Luther, Pestalozzi reached down below the housefathers to the very bottom of the social ladder and granted religious autonomy to poor women. In doing so he democratized religion far more radically than did Luther.

No great social philosophy then or later theorized the political implications of this sort of transfer of religious autonomy. Not even Marx. He related the Lutheran affirmation of religious autonomy to the theory of political autonomy, which brought about the "philosophical transformation of priestly Germans into men." [13] He recognized that Luther's transfer of religious authority had only produced what he called "lay popes—the princes together with their clergy [wealthy aristocrats], the privileged and the philistines." [14] But he thought that a philosophy of political autonomy, of a fundamental human right to freedom, would transform "the priestly Germans into men," that is, into men like all other men, and thus help to "emancipate the people." [15] Nonetheless, Marx recognized that philosophical theory is not enough to bring about a radical revolution. "Revolutions require a passive element, a material base," which for him was the developing proletariat.[16] As he put it, "The head of emancipation is philosophy, its heart is the proletariat." [17] But Marx did not look closely at the mothers of the proletariat, nor did he speculate about the alternate philosophy of freedom implied in the transfer of religious autonomy to women's souls. Perhaps as his use

of heart imagery suggests, he ignored the alternate philosophy because he saw the potential oppressiveness of
representations of feminine souls. He may have equated
the representations of the feminine soul current in his
time with the normalized psyche of the bourgeois housewife. Again, he may have been unable to use his imagination to turn representations of the feminine soul of
poor mothers like Gertrude into real Gertrudes who produced people with caring labor. He too may have wondered what these mothers did with their children until
they were six or seven.

For whatever reason, no great thinker theorized the
revolutionary implications of Gertrude's religious autonomy. Most especially, progressive German men who
saw themselves as the modern heirs of Luther did not
theorize the revolutionary implications of women's religious autonomy. Only Pestalozzi tried to draw out the
social and political implications of his representation of
the religious autonomy of woman's soul in a later work.

THE THREAT TO MAN'S
POLITICAL AUTONOMY

The conduct of Gertrude in Pestalozzi's tale posed an
equal challenge to men's perception of themselves as politically autonomous beings, a philosophy that was relatively young but nonetheless firmly embedded in European thought. In *In a Different Voice,* Carol Gilligan
explains that the moral ideal of autonomy is expressed
in a "concept of a separate self or of moral principles
uncompromised by the constraints of reality" as an ado-
lescent ideal.[18] She writes, "To admit the truth of the
women's perspective to the concept of moral development is to recognize for both sexes the importance
throughout life of the connection between self and other,
the universality of the need for compassion and care." [19]

The giant political theoreticians of what Hester
Eisenstein calls the Western liberal political tradition,
including the German philosophers of autonomy, clearly

recognized that their theories of the moral development
of political man had to account for the connection between self and other. Rousseau and many of his German
heirs through Marx thought that man could only become
man, that is, fully human and therefore fully free, in
interaction with other humans. Further, the individual
man, the separate self, could only become fully free in a
community in which his will was in unity with those of
all others. All these philosophers understood that *somehow* this interaction and unity with the other had to be
more than a spiritual unity. The interaction with others
involved the constraints of reality in the sense of a relation to physical and material conditions. Most clearly,
this interaction involved men's property. But some, including Rousseau, even saw the universality of the need
for compassion and love. As we saw in chapter 2, Rousseau even thought that breast-feeding was a condition for
social unity, but he based this judgment on a crude belief
that located hereditary moral characteristics of good men
in good women's milk. Nonetheless, a basic premise of
the humanitarian reformers who tried to develop a theory
of punishment on the basis of the new political theory
was the need for compassion and a new sort of care for
souls.

The preeminent German philosophers of freedom,
Immanuel Kant, G. W. F. Hegel, and Johann Fichte,
were preoccupied with identifying the conditions necessary for realizing a community of free individuals, that is,
the type of interaction between humans that could make
men truly human and free. But to find these conditions,
they looked inward into what characterized men as human—their capacity for thought or self-reflection. Their
rationale was that only by looking at man's most intrinsic
or innate quality could they identify what was truly universal, common to all men beneath their external differences. When the term *idealist* is used in the German
context, it refers to this turn inward to self-reflection or,
as it is more often called, self-consciousness, in order to

discover the true and universal basis of human community.

We may describe the efforts of these men in another way. We may say that they tried to define an innate principle of man's freedom from external authority and at the same time to show that duty or responsibility to others was the innately free man's highest good. Kant was the first to define this innate principle. He tried to show that duty or responsibility to others was man's highest good precisely because man possessed a moral autonomy. According to Kant, the conscience of every man was guided by the innate imperative to regard himself and to treat every other man as an end, not as a means. Thus, man's conscience was guided by an innate spiritual, in the sense of mental, principle of universal justice. Man's moral autonomy is itself the ground of a just social and political order because each man's conscience tells him that he has the right to be a subject *and* the duty to treat all others as subjects. No man, king or otherwise, has the right to turn other men into objects, means, or mere things.

Kant and Fichte, and Hegel after him, knew there were problems in applying this universal principle of justice under the constraints of reality or the real world, where men brought their bodies and their possessions along with their consciences. To solve these problems, Kant turned to religion as one solution. He conjectured that since in the world of everyday life, of a life bound to earthly needs, the principle of universal justice is never perfectly realized, the rational autonomous man needs the *hypotheses* of the existence of a just God and of the immortality of the soul in order to motivate himself to continue to act according to his conscience. In the face of immediate imperfections of justice, he needs to think that justice is a real ideal existing in God's heaven and that someday he will participate in that heaven through an immortal soul. For Kant, this belief in the existence of a just God and his kingdom is a *rational* illusion. Kant's God is not the traditional God of the housefathers; their God was believed to be a transcendent God in the sense of actually existing beyond the human mind and the material world. This new God of autonomous man is called transcendental in the sense of a necessary hypothesis on which the possibility of moral behavior is grounded. Nonetheless, even without his transcendence, Kant's God retains the character of a just father.

Pestalozzi had his own answers for the questions posed by Kant and continually pondered by the later German idealist political philosophers. Pestalozzi wrote, "Ask the good man, 'Why is duty your highest good? Why do you believe in God?' If he gives you proofs, only the schools are speaking in him. A more skillful intellect beats all these proofs down. He trembles a moment, but his heart cannot deny the Divine; he comes back to him, blessing and loving as to his mother's bosom." [20]

The mother's breast, not the universal principle of justice, grounded Pestalozzi's theories of both duty and God. To the question on the ground of social and political communities, he answered, "They have their chief source in the relations that exist between the baby and the mother." [21]

Pestalozzi's Defense of Gertrude's Soul

In *How Gertrude Teaches Her Children,* Pestalozzi reported that he discovered the way to explore the higher realm of morality, not by turning inward and using reflection, but through an encounter with a young child. "[I] forgot the judgments of God and of men and experienced the bliss of human nature and its sacred innocence while losing, or finding, myself in the child on my knees. . . . So a deep feeling of love which was stronger than everything that troubled me, saved me from utter ruin." [22]

Pestalozzi drew out the meaning of this deep feeling of love by changing the soul of Gertrude. No longer merely the source of physical and moral order as in *Leonard and Gertrude,* in *How Gertrude Teaches Her Children* Gertrude's soul becomes the source of all moral development and the mirror of a new God—God the mother.

In a startling departure from the philosophers of autonomy, Pestalozzi claimed that conditions for the possibility of human morality were to be found in the relationship with the mother. The bases of morality are love, trust, and gratitude, not fear of the Lord or the rational belief in his kingdom of justice, and the three bases appear in embryonic form in the early relationship of the mother and child. Like Gilligan, Pestalozzi recognized the centrality of love to moral development and the role of women in providing and developing love through their social function as mothers. But he went still further. Like the radical women-centered feminists, he drove the link between women and mortality deep into women's bodies. With an undeniable but highly psychological biologism that clearly anticipated Freud's, Pestalozzi wrote, "The mother is forced by the power of animal instinct to tend her child, feed him, protect and please him. She does this. She satisfies his wants, she removes anything unpleasant, she comes to the help of his helplessness. The child is cared for, is pleased. *The germ of love is developed in him."* The germ of trust is developed by the mother when she calms the child's fear of the strange new world. When the child is frightened by new objects, she holds it close, soothes it, and smiles at it. The child "returns his mother's smile with clear unclouded eyes." [23] The germ of gratitude is developed when the mother responds to the child's need for nourishment with her breast. "His eye is cast on her breast. He is satisfied. Mother, and being satisfied, are one and the same thought to him." [24]

Duty as the human's highest good is rooted in the

early relationship of mother and child. Acceptance of duty or obedience is, Pestalozzi acknowledged, "opposed to the first inclinations of animal nature." Nonetheless, obedience is closely related to instinct and "its first stage is distinctly instinctive." He explained, "As *want* precedes love, *nourishment* gratitude, care trust, so *passionate desire* precedes obedience." This is a passionate desire for the mother's breast, for which the child must learn to wait until she offers it to him. Through this waiting the child learns patience, the prerequisite of obedience, a passive obedience derived from "a consciousness of hard necessity." Pestalozzi wrote, "*Active* obedience develops much later, and later still, the consciousness that it is good for him to obey the mother." [25]

In an extraordinary paragraph Pestalozzi summarized his "first principles of moral self-development," which he found, not in the inner regions of self-consciousness, but in observing and remembering the "strong passionate desire for the satisfaction of physical wants," which unfold in "the natural relations between mother and child." [26]

> Obedience and love, gratitude and trust united, develop the first germ of conscience, the first faint shadow of the feeling that *it is not right* to rage against the loving mother; the first faint shadow of the feeling that the mother is not in the world *altogether for his sake;* the first faint shadow of the feeling that everything in the world is not altogether for his sake; and with it is also germinated the feeling that *he himself* is not in the world for *his own sake* only. The first shadow of duty and right is in the germ.[27]

In this theory of moral development, it is the child's intimate and satisfying knowledge of the mother that leads him to treat others as ends and not means. The child learns in relation to the mother to love those who are "like her; a creature like its mother is a good creature to him." He learns to love those his mother loves. *"The germ of human love, of brotherly love is developed in him."* [28]

It is not merely morality that is engendered by the passionate desire for the mother's breast and the dynamic of the interaction of mother and child. Religion is also engendered here. Like Kant, Pestalozzi viewed religion as the ultimate guarantor of morality, but unlike Kant he did not consider God a rational illusion. Pestalozzi declared, "The germ of all feelings of dependence on God, through faith, is in its essence, the same germ which is produced by the infant's dependence on its mother." The true and higher faith in God emerges later, with the consciousness of the child's separate personality, with the secret thought *"I no longer need my mother."* [29]

When the child discovers this, he does not follow the path assumed by male thinkers: He does not turn to the father or his governmental substitutes as a model for personality and ultimately for an image of God. Pestalozzi found another path, and through this he presented a pre-Oedipal theology. The mother steps in and makes what men would find a threatening move to forestall the expected path of spiritual development. Recognizing the child's growing sense of separation, she "presses her darling more firmly to her heart." [30]

Holding her child close, the mother gives him religious instruction. She says, "in a voice [he] has not yet heard, 'Child, there is a God whom thou needest, who taketh thee in His arms when thou needest me no longer, when I can shelter thee no more. There is a God who prepares joy and happiness for thee when I can no more give them thee." [31] The voice the child has not yet heard is the voice of authority, a voice making the authoritative claim that God is like the speaker. Upon hearing her words, the child feels "an inexpressible something" rise in his heart and the "feelings of love, gratitude and trust that were developed at her bosom, extend and embrace God as a father, God as a mother." [32]

According to this theology, for God to be a father
and for men to be fathers like him is for them to be like
the mother. Being like the mother and staying in relation
to the mother provide the religious ground for morality.
With the emergence of belief in God who is like the
mother, the child can fully recognize duty as the highest
good. "The child who believes from this time forwards in
the eye of God as in the eye of his mother, does right
now for *God's sake,* as he formerly did for his *mother's
sake.*" [33]

PESTALOZZI'S THEOLOGY IN
THE COMMUNITY

Morality and religion both begin in "the *coincidence
of instinctive feelings* between mother and child." Both
have their origins in the instinctive sensuous relation
between mother and child. But their development is
dependent on human art, not physical instinct. And as
we might guess, Pestalozzi described this as a female art,
the art of spinning. Moral development requires the
art of holding the threads of the feelings of morality
and religion running through the web of life *by remembering their origin.* Only if these threads remain attached
to that original coincidence of instinctive feelings between mother and child after the child separates from the
mother, only if they remain attached to that "golden
spindle of creation," can the human develop fully.[34]

With increasing independence and a sense of his
own powers, the child is drawn away from the mother
into what Pestalozzi characterized as a corrupt and dangerous world. He lamented, "Mother, mother! He has
lost you, he has lost God, he has lost himself. The touch
of love is quenched for him. The germ of *self-respect* is
dead within him. He is going towards destruction, striving only after sensual enjoyment." [35] A sensuous touch,
the intimate touching of mother and child, plants in
human conscience the germ of self-respect, that funda-

mental sense that one ought not to treat oneself as a thing, as a means, but as a subject and an end. When the human loses the feeling of *this* sensuous touching, he abandons himself to "sensual enjoyment," to being a thing or an object.

Pestalozzi argued that the crucial moment in moral development is the "moment of transition between the feelings of trust in the mother and God, and those of trust in the new aspect of the world." [36] What is crucial, therefore, is retaining the relation to the mother (which is the relation to God) and transfering this relation to human activity in the larger world. Here there is no wrenching away from the mother and no transfer of affection to the father. This is not necessary, because true fathers and God himself act like mothers.[37]

Pestalozzi expressed his pre-Oedipal theology in a simple prayer: "Mother! I can keep my innocence, my love, my obedience, the excellence of my nobler nature with the new impressions of the world, *all, all* at *your side only.* . . . Mother, mother! we will not *part from each other* at the moment when I run into danger of being drawn away from you, from God, and from myself, by the new phenomena of the world. Mother, mother! *sanctify the transition from your heart to this world, by the support of your heart.*" [38]

The integration of self-development with life in community, which the giants of German idealism pondered deeply, is made possible, according to Pestalozzi, through mother love. Whereas Kant proposed a rational hypothesis of the existence of God in order to assure moral behavior, Pestalozzi proposed the intense feelings in the relationship between *mother* and *child;* these feelings reveal the truth of God the mother. In religious feeling, "mother and Creator, mother and Preserver, become . . . one and the same emotion for the child.' [39] Pestalozzi's description of the social consequences of belief in the mother as Creator is strikingly different from the images presented by the German idealist philosophers of autonomy. Like other thinkers, Fichte found it thoroughly "confusing."

I will quote at length Pestalozzi's description of mother and preserver being one.

> [Through this religion of the mother the man becomes] the father of the poor, the support of the wretched. As my mother *leaves* her healthy children and *clings* to the sickly, and *takes double care* of the wretched because she *must, being the mother,* because she stands in God's place to the child, so must *I, if the mother is in God's place* to me, and God fills my heart in the *mother's place.* A feeling like the mother's feeling impels me. Man is my brother, my love embraces the whole race, but I cling to the *wretched,* I am *doubly* his father; to act *like God* [like the mother] becomes my *nature.* I am a child of God; I believed in my mother, her heart showed me God. God is the God of my *mother,* of *my heart* and *her heart.* I know no other God. The God of my *brain* is a *chimaera.* I know no other God but the God of my *heart.* By faith in the God of *my heart* only I feel like a man. The God of my *brain* is an *idol.* I ruin myself by worshipping him. The God of my *heart* is my God. I perfect myself in His love. Mother, mother! you showed me God in your *commands,* and I found Him in *obedience.* Mother, mother! when I forget *God* I forget *you,* and when I *love* God I am in *your place* to the infant. I cling to your *wretched ones,* and *those who weep,* rest in my arms as in their *mother's.*
>
> Mother, mother! as I love you so I love God, and duty is *my highest good.* Mother! when *I forget you, I forget* God.... Then live I like the lion, for *myself* and in self-confidence use my powers for *myself against my own race.* Then there is no sense of fatherhood in my soul, then *no sense of God* sanctifies my obedience; and my apparent *sense of duty* is a vain deception. Mother, mother! as I love you, so I love God. *Mother* and *obedience, God* and

duty are one and the same to me—*God's will,* and the *best* and *noblest,* that I can imagine, are one and the same to me. I live then no more for *myself;* I lose myself in *my brethren,* the children of my God—I live *no more for myself,* I live for Him who took me in my mother's arms, and *raised* me with a father's hand above the dust of my mortal coil to His love. And the more I love Him, the Eternal, the more I honour His commandments, the more I *depend on Him,* the more I *lose myself and become His,* the more does my nature become *divine,* the more do I feel in harmony with my inner nature and with my whole race." [40]

FURTHER IMPLICATIONS OF GERTRUDE'S SOUL

In making Gertrude's soul the basis of a higher moral theory, in intensifying its religious qualities, and finally in describing God in its image, Pestalozzi changed it. No longer was it merely an internal mirror of the proper external order. Gertrude's soul took on a life of its own. It became a psychobiological essence, reaching on one side to the divine and on the other into the female body.

In *Leonard and Gertrude,* Gertrude's soul, although the source of her proper mothering, was gender neutral. It inspired her to give the physical energy that costs nothing and to use her body to reproduce good subjects, but it was not intrinsically tied to her body. It was rather a clear mirror of the order of the father's kingdom. Thus the qualities of order in her soul could have been, and were supposed to be, transferred to the souls of not only her children but also Leonard. In fact, the minister who became a schoolteacher, Gluelphi, discovers quickly how to have her soul, and although Pestalozzi did not allow Gertrude's soul to fade from prominence in Bonnal, it is clear that Gluelphi and his male disciples could have carried on without her once they had removed the children from the home. The religious qualities of order, though serving to make Gertrude a good mother, were separable from her body and her gender; they remained the qualities necessary for order in a father's kingdom.

By contrast, Gertrude's new intensely religious soul in *How Gertrude Teaches Her Children,* a soul that reflects God the mother, is not gender neutral. Like the genius described by Rich, it is the soul of a biological female, of a body that gives birth and nourishes the infant. Yet its qualities could and were supposed to be transferred to men, transferred when men are infants at the breast. With this assertion, Pestalozzi did not repeat the crude biologism of Rousseau. Pestalozzi's biologism was both psychological and theological. For him, the religious soul of woman grounding all moral development reached from her body to God, to ultimate reality itself, which is also a mother, nurturing her child at the breast.

Fichte's Suppression of Gertrude's Soul

In *Of Woman Born* Rich examines Freud's description of the Oedipus complex and asks whether the male child's separation from the mother means that the child must "'join the army.'" [41] Does this separation mean that the male must internalize the values of the father in a male-dominated society? Pestalozzi answered no; the boy can internalize the values of his loving mother. Johann Fichte, Germany's philosopher of autonomy who was the most enthusiastic and influential admirer of Pestalozzi, gave an unequivocally different reponse; he answered yes, of course.

Fichte gave that answer while proposing in his famous *Addresses to the German Nation* that Pestalozzi's methods of education be adopted as the model for the type of education that should be undertaken in Germany on a national scale. The translator of the *Addresses* claims that they mark "an epoch in the history of the world," because "the principle of [German] national unity" espoused by Fichte, the "apostle of the gospel" of liberty, equality, and brotherhood among men, "had far-reaching effects on the political development of Europe in the nineteenth century." [42] Fichte delivered these addresses in the winter of 1807 to large audiences in Berlin, the capital of Prussia, when that state and most of the rest of German territory was under French occupation. Napoleon's army invaded Germany in 1805, occupied Berlin in 1806, and won enormous concessions from Prussia in 1807 in the Treaty of Tilsit. This largest and strongest of the German Protestant states lost vast amounts of land and money and, most importantly, the strength of its noted professional army. Noted, that is, not only for its discipline and valor but also for its seduction of innocent girls. When Fichte spoke, soldiers from Napoleon's army were quartered in Berlin. The freedom-lover Fichte took it upon himself to raise the morale of the German people and to outwit the forces of occupation by offering the German states a new and unexpected way to enable all men to "join the army"—through a national system of education. A national education would be the defensive strategy that would ensure the preservation of "German individuality and German love of the fatherland" in the face of conquest.[43] Fichte insisted that the establishment of a system of national education was not an impractical dream, because its beginnings already existed in "the system of instruction invented and proposed by Johann Heinrich Pestalozzi, and already practiced under his eyes." [44] Fichte was referring to the school Pestalozzi founded in 1774, and claimed that this system "might, indeed, have the power of helping . . . the whole human race to rise from the depths of its present misery." [45]

What could have been a greater affirmation? Fichte had read *Leonard and Gertrude* in 1788, met Pestalozzi in 1793, and read *How Gertrude Teaches Her Children* in 1805 when the French invasion forced him to leave his post as a philosophy professor. But despite all this study and his high praise for Pestalozzi's system of education, Fichte had trouble with the educator's two versions of the soul of Gertrude. He could not believe in either version. He thought the representations of Gertrude's

soul were too materialistic to embody the moral and
spiritual perfection of German individuality. They were
the wrong representations for inspiring German men to
form a moral army.[46]

Fichte's rejection of the real Gertrudes of this world
was complete. "First of all, so far as this home education
is concerned, we have certainly no desire to quarrel with
[Pestalozzi] over the hopes he forms of mothers. But, so
far as *our higher conception* of a national education is
concerned, we are firmly convinced that, especially among
the working classes, it cannot be either begun, continued,
or ended in the parents' house, nor, indeed without *the
complete separation* of the children from them. The hardship, the daily anxiety about making ends meet, the
petty meanness and avarice, which occur here, would inevitably infect the children, drag them down, and prevent them from making a free flight into the world of
thought." [47]

Fichte was convinced that the mothers of the people
could only reproduce the given condition of faltering
spirituality, of the inability to take flight into the world
of thought, which was necessary to his higher conception
of education. He had "seen enough of what will happen
if mankind as a whole repeats itself in each successive
generation as it has in the previous one. If its complete
reformation is intended, [this generation] must once and
for all be entirely separated from itself and cut off altogether from its old life. Not until a generation has
passed through the new education can the question be
considered, as to what part of the national education
shall be entrusted to the home." [48]

This pedagogy of separation from the mother made
real Gertrudes unimaginable. It allows only for women
who are characterized by pettiness and avarice, women
who are drags on the free flight of thought—a familiar
but not original image. In posing her question about
boys' having to "join the army," Rich also wonders
whether the mother can represent culture in a male-

dominated society. Fichte declared no; mothers, indeed all mothers and not just mothers of the poor, can only reproduce the given conditions of society. Mothers and the materialism they represent are the enemies of cultural revolution. Mothers, as de Beauvoir said, are thieves of time.[49] Thus the first step in the reform of the nation is to entirely separate this generation from its mothers.

Fichte arrived at these conclusions after studying Pestalozzi because he is above all else a master of German idealism and a believer in the autonomous ego. Fichte appealed to the existence of Pestalozzi's system of education only to prove to his German audiences that a national system of education was possible. He argued that the existence of a model for a kind of mass education demonstrated that his own scheme for reform through education was not merely "a picture set up for the exercise of ingenuity of mind" but could rather "be put into practice" at once.[50] In pointing out that a system had been "already successfully practiced under the eyes" of Pestalozzi, Fichte defended his own realism.[51] But then he became the idealist. He reported that although he had met Pestalozzi and read his books, he did not take a good look at his school. This, said Fichte, was certainly not because he did not admire this educator's system of education, but because he wanted to get a "definite and clear conception of Pestalozzi's true intention first.[52] Why? Because the actual practice may not match the intention. For Fichte, the ideal, in this instance Pestalozzi's true intention, was the real; therefore, to ensure that his system of education will be the right one, the real one, Fichte set out first to clarify Pestalozzi's intentions. Only after that clarification was made could he put Pestalozzi's theory into practice. In the process of making this clarification, Fichte eliminated Pestalozzi's two representations of Gertrude's soul.

What he found right about Pestalozzi's intention was, not surprisingly, what Fichte judged to be consistent with Luther's intention. This was the intention to "stimu-

late and train the free activity of the pupil's mind" and
to free that mind of "mist and shadows." [53] Luther did
this by freeing German men from the religion of Rome,
its superstitions and its oppressive political authority.
Pestalozzi did this by leading children "to direct perception." [54] Certainly, his depiction of the debilitating
influence of Hubel-Rudy's wife's dreams on her children
and her children's salvation by Gertrude, who teaches
them to be observant of what is around them, should
have appealed to Fichte. Pestalozzi's intention did, but
his representation of Gertrude's soul did not. The philosopher said, without a qualm, that Pestalozzi was unable to express his own intention and thus he himself
must describe what it really is. Fichte cloaked his suppression of the feminine soul in an apparent clarification of the goals of a system of national education.

MORAL EDUCATION

In his definition of the purpose of national education,
Fichte revealed his interpretation of the intent he read
into *Leonard and Gertrude.* He wrote, national education "must consist completely in this, that it completely
destroys freedom of the will in the soil which it under-
takes to cultivate and produces on the contrary strict
necessity in the decisions of the will." [55] This education
will produce a stable character in its pupils, which "cannot be other than it is." [56] This character will shape a
man so that he "cannot will otherwise than you wish him
to will." [57] It will allow the teacher to inscribe on men's
souls, as Gluelphi learned to do, the order necessary for
the good society.

As a true philosopher of autonomy, Fichte believed
that the exercise of this constraint through education was
consistent with man's freedom. It was consistent with the
affirmation of man's innate freedom and goodness. Until
Pestalozzi, education of the common people had been
the responsibility of Christian ministers, who had wrongly
assumed the truth of Original Sin, that is, that "everyone
loves and wills his own material welfare." [58] Thus these

men and the Church used threats and promises to try to
maintain order in society and to instill in men a sense
of the common good; they also used theaters of hell.
But like Pestalozzi and other reformers, Fichte thought
that this mode of moral education left men bad *inwardly*.
A new form of moral education was necessary to "mold
men who are inwardly and fundamentally good since it
is through such men alone that the German nation can
still continue to exist, whereas through bad men it will
inevitably be absorbed in the outside world." [59] It will
inevitably remain subjugated to France.

According to Fichte, Christian educators lacked a
proper understanding of man's will. They did not realize
that man "can will only what he loves." [60] In order to
combat a selfish, materialistic love, educators must create in men a love that takes the "form of a pleasure
so intense that a man is thereby stimulated to realize the
good in his life." This intense pleasure will constitute
the basis of the "pupil's stable and constant character." [61]
In *How Gertrude Teaches Her Children,* Pestalozzi also
identified pleasure as the basis of a stable and constant
character—the pleasure of the infant fed at the breast.
Experiencing this pleasure, "Mother, and being satisfied"
become "one and the same thought" to the child.[62] But
Pestalozzi did not know how to express his intention
and he certainly did not know how to identify real pleasure, according to Fichte.

Fichte defined real pleasure as that which stimulates
man to make real his ideals. Thus it presupposes "an
image of that state, which, previous to its actual existence, hovers before the mind." [63] The images in the
mind, mental ideals, produce a pleasure so intense that
men are stimulated to make them real. And it is in the
action of making them real that a man knows what it is
to be free and self-determining. He knows the pleasure of
possessing an ego.

That man can have this kind of pleasure and stimulation from images and ideals presupposes that he "has
the power to create spontaneously such images, which

are independent of reality and not copies of it, but rather its prototypes." [64] It presupposes that men can create spontaneously in their minds models of what life ought to be and that these models can then stimulate him to make them real. What could be a purer freedom? Men can make up images and ideals that have social and material power.

The recognition of this potential in man was the "starting point for moulding" the German people by education.[65] Pestalozzi's contribution was to see that these models or prototypes of what life ought to be cannot merely be impressed on the minds of men by others. Men cannot merely be presented with the proper representations. They must create them themselves because having a sense of self-activity in generating them is essential to produce in man the pleasure that stimulates him to make them real.

The fundamental pedagogical problem is how to educate men to spontaneously generate these prototypes. How do teachers educate men to take free flights of thought? Pestalozzi's answer was simple: Stimulate "this personal activity in the pupil" by training the child in direct perception of the world around him.[66] Do not subject him to memorizing the words of others. For the idealist, training the child in direct perception is the same as stimulating the child's mind to create its own images. For the idealist, these images are not copies of reality. They are not merely the impression on the mind of what is perceived, but the production of the mind, of the imagination.

Fichte argued that this stimulation of the pleasures of using the imagination can lead men to make real a good society, a community of wills, because all men, when properly stimulated, will imagine the same thing. Why? Because they are all the same. In the inner regions of their true selves, in their self-consciousnesses, in their egos, there are universal and "infallible laws." [67] This view goes back to Kant, who thought that the universal law of justice was innate in man's conscience. Fichte believed in similar mental laws *and* in the power of men's wills to make them real. He believed that men would spontaneously imagine the *same* prototypes of society. Thus the imagination, rather than being dangerous, could be controlled by educators like him and indeed by the state itself. When properly educated, men would find it impossible to imagine the wrong idea.

Fichte made extraordinary claims for men's minds. He insisted that "the eternal, universal, and fundamental law of man's mental nature" is "that he must directly engage in mental activity." [68] In fact, man's true nature is to be self-consciously reflective. Men have an innate taste for the infinite and eternal. Men who are selfish, or materialistic, are not "natural" men; they are men oppressed by "immediate necessity and present material need." [69] Obviously natural men cannot live where the "hardship, the daily anxiety about making ends meet, the petty meanness and avarice, which occur here, would inevitably infect [them], drag them down, and prevent them from making a free flight into the world of thought." [70] Obviously, they must be separated from their mothers. It is only when men have taken care of their immediate needs that they can take their natural "poetic flight to ideal worlds." [71] They need an education that will result even from its very beginnings "in knowledge which transcends all experience, which is abstract, absolute, and strictly universal, and which includes within itself beforehand all subsequently possible experience." [72] Imagine. The images created in men's poetic flights to ideal worlds include all subsequently possible experience.

Fichte carried his reasoning to its logical conclusions. He declared that it is not good for boys to have their "natural freedom from care" repressed or for men to be prudent.[73] In the end, Fichte did not think it wise for men in the army to marry or be attached to their mothers.

SIGNS, READING, AND WOMEN

Fichte thought it unwise to let mothers teach their babies how to read. Here he may have uncovered a truth. De-

spite Pestalozzi's negative representation of the effects of
reading on Hubel-Rudy's wife in *Leonard and Gertrude,*
Fichte insisted that Pestalozzi did not fully realize the
dangers of reading and writing. He did not see that reading and writing have been "the very instruments for en-
veloping men in mist and shadow" and for making them
selfish.[74] Clearly he did not see the danger in good mothers like Gertrude teaching reading and writing to their
children. In effect, he did not see that reading and writing are too materialistic to be part of early childhood
education.

How could mothers teaching their children the alphabet be dangerous to men and to their society? According to Fichte, the teaching of reading and writing can
lead the child astray from "direct perception to mere
signs, and from attention, which knows that it grasps
nothing if it does not grasp it now and here, to distrac-
tion, which consoles itself by writing things down and
wants to learn some day from paper what it will probably
never learn, and, in general, to the dreaming which so
often accompanies dealings with the letters of the alphabet." [75] This is a remarkable assertion: Written, material signs are not reliable. When one goes back to
them after time to learn from the paper on which they
are written, the truth of immediate experience is lost.
This is again the voice of the idealist: The truth of immediate experience is not the true impression of the
thing perceived, but the production in the mind of universal laws. The signs of writing threaten this production.
The signs of writing can get out of hand; they can vio-
late the universal laws of the mind.

To understand this view, we might imagine a young
child freely playing with alphabet blocks, making up
"words" with them and thinking the combination of letters represents something the child is imagining. But even
hitting on real words in this play would lead straight to
the world of shadow and mist, according to Fichte. Word
signs add nothing to the clarity of inner knowledge. We
need them only for communication with others, not for

the production of knowledge itself. Until children are educated in direct perception, only dreaming can result from dealing with the letters of the alphabet. One can only wonder what all those hours of mothers' play with alphabet blocks have done to boys. Fichte held that they have distracted boys from their fathers' wills and truths, and thus the signs of writing must not be used by young children—or perhaps even by mothers. Fichte was so distressed by the danger of material signs that he declared that everything Pestalozzi said "about sound and words as the means for the development of mental powers" was wrong.[76] Immediately after this condemnation he insisted that children be separated from their mothers in the new, true national system of education.

The dangers in mothers' teaching of signs and even mothers' sounds in baby talk are associated by Fichte with the danger of women's bodies. Amazingly he seems to have hit on the truth proclaimed by contemporary French feminists that not only women's writing out of their physical experience but also the language that characterizes the baby's early relation with the mother, rhythmic babble, is dangerous in man's world.[77] Here woman and baby play with signs and do not respect a rule that they should be used only to strictly represent the intentions and the truth of the father. The two ignore the warning that only the laws of the father's world should be represented in language.

Fichte's position will become clearer if we contrast his views on the scholar and writing with his views on mothers and baby talk. Only those who intend to be scholars should be taught to write before the very end of their education, because only they "by solitary reflection" can "lift up into the light of language the hidden and real depths of . . . audible thought." [78] Writing should be men's audible thought, their expression of "their feeling about what is universally valid." [79] Writing should be controlled to represent the images and prototypes men spontaneously create.

Even speech, the material sign of sound, should be

men's audible thought about the universally true, and
hence there should be no baby talk. "When the child begins to understand, and imperfectly to make, speech
sounds, he should be led to make himself quite clear,
whether he is hungry or sleepy, whether he sees or hears
the actual sensation denoted by this or that expression,
or indeed, simply imagines it. He should be clear, too,
as to the differences and degrees of difference of the various impressions on the same sense that are denoted by
special words, e.g., colours and the sounds of different
bodies, etc." [80] Imagine. Mothers should wait to respond
to their barely verbal babies' needs until those babes
clearly express just what need they have and to what degree. And, by all means, they should not enjoy, encourage, and imitate the beauty of the baby's sounds by joining in the babble.

What does this restraint on the part of mothers ac-
complish? "By this means the child first obtains an ego,
which he abstracts in free and conscious conception, and
which he scrutinizes by its aid: as soon as it awakes to
life, a mental eye is set in life, and from that time on-
ward never leaves it." [81] It allows the child to learn reflection, to use its own innate mental eye. Obviously, it
also would keep the child from confusing this eye with
the eye of his mother, which Pestalozzi equated with
God's eye as the foundation for all duty. It would also
keep the child from being too satisfied and from finding
a model for responsibility in the mother's anticipation of
need through her love. Then too in forcing the child to
tie down his desire to a specified and quantified need, it
might teach the child not to miss the mother love Pestalozzi described.

Fichte called this teaching of exact speech the
A B C's of sensation. The development of the ego involves
a discipline of the senses, a tying down of desire, and a
knowledge of how to control the body. And, of course, it
involves a separation from the mother's body. Just after
he stated that children must be separated from their

mothers if national education were to succeed, Fichte wrote, "[Setting aside Pestalozzi's false hope for mothers], and considering [his] book for mothers simply as the first foundation of instruction; to take, as the book does, the child's body as the subject of instruction is also a complete mistake. [Pestalozzi] starts with the very correct statement, that the first object of the child's knowledge must be the child himself. But is the child's body, then, the child himself?" [82] No, the child himself is the ego, the self.

Fichte then identified the real danger of any home education. If the first object of a child's knowledge must be a human body, "would not the mother's body be far closer and more visible to him [than his own]?" [83] Yes, and that is why education cannot begin with the body. To allow the sight or touch of the mother's body, the sounds of her rhythmic baby talk, or even her play with alphabet blocks to be the foundation for the moral education of modern men would, thought Fichte, be a complete mistake.

Fichte's reinterpretation of Pestalozzi's intent may leave the reader believing that he rejected every facet of the educator's theory of the child's early training. But he did agree with one of Pestalozzi's views. He approved of the method of strict physical exercise to turn the body into the perfect machine that it is. Fichte particularly liked one line from Pestalozzi that captured this method: "Striking, carrying, throwing, pushing, pulling, turning, struggling, swinging, etc., are the simplest exercises of strength." [84]

THE SUPPRESSION OF GOD THE MOTHER

Finally, Fichte took issue with Pestalozzi's association of God, mother, and brotherly love. The philosopher commented, "Pestalozzi speaks of this subject with soul-stirring enthusiasm. Yet we must confess that his statements do not seem at all clear to us, and least of all, so clear that they could serve as the foundation for an art of developing love. It is therefore necessary for us to state our own thoughts concerning such a foundation." [85] Fichte then presented his view. "The bond . . . which makes men of one mind, and the development of which is a chief part of education for manhood, is not sensuous love, but the instinct for mutual respect." [86] Sensuous love, those intimate and early touches of love between mother and child, cannot arouse the instinct for self or mutual respect.

Fichte agreed with Pestalozzi that the instinct for self-respect and respect of others as selves is the root of a healthy and free people, a strong, modern society. He also agreed that the first appearance of this instinct for respect in the child is manifest as desire. But the two writers disagreed on the object of that desire. For Pestalozzi the instinct for respect appeared first as the child's passionate desire for the breast. This in turn means that mothers are the ones who inspire respect in the child by their love of him and of others. Fichte made a similar formulation, but reached a different conclusion. For him, this instinct "appears first of all as the desire to be respected by those who inspire in him the highest respect." [87] And this person is the father.

Despite his professed intellectual advances in the science of morals and society, Fichte repeated an old story, the housefather tale: "This instinct [for self-respect in the child] goes to prove with certainty that love does not arise from selfishness at all, because it is directed as a rule far more strongly and decisively towards the sterner parent, the father, who is more often absent, and who does not appear directly as a benefactor, than towards the mother, who with her beneficence is ever present. The child wants to be noticed by him, wants to have his approval; only in so far as the father is satisfied with him is he satisfied with himself." [88] Mother and being satisfied are not one and the same for Fichte. He could not understand Pestalozzi on this. He could not imagine it.

Fichte, the philosopher of revolution, restored the original version of the housefather's story, which Pestalozzi's two volumes on Gertrude's soul had distorted. This idealist suppressed Pestalozzi's identification of mother love and God, and returned mother love to its earlier status as a low, nearly subhuman form of love, an animal instinct that can satisfy only physical needs. Only fathers can give real love, the kind that binds society together: "[The instinct for self-respect] is the natural love of the child for the father, not as the guardian of his sensuous well-being, but as the mirror, from which his own worth or worthlessness is reflected for him. Now, the father himself can easily connect with this love obedience and every kind of self-denial; for the reward of his hearty approval the child obeys with joy." [89] By serving as the rewarding and punishing judge of his child's behavior, the father instills true morality in the child. By acting like God the father and judge in much of Christian belief, the father can connect love and obedience and every kind of self-denial.

Thus it is the sight of the father's love, not the touch of the mother's love, that "animates and strengthens the child's love" and ensures the child's self-control.[90] This all makes sense to Fichte because for him love "is the essential element in man; it exists, as a man exists, whole and complete, and nothing can be added to it, for it transcends the growing phenomenon of the sensuous life, and is independent of it." [91]

Fichte had a total aversion to Pestalozzi's representation of woman's soul, a soul that extended, on the one hand, to the maternal body and, on the other hand, to God the mother. Further, he could not believe in the reality of the educator's representation of woman's soul as the source of order in the father's kingdom. This rejection of the representation of religious qualities in the feminine soul not only recalls the Christian theology of Eve but also seems prophetic. Certainly, Fichte could not stretch his powerful imagination to clarify Pestalozzi's pre-Oedipal morality or theology. Instead, he defined a father who, like the father in Freud's Oedipal theory, has a mantle of authority and a quality of physical strength even before the child and father get entangled with the mother. Fichte's analysis makes us wonder if Freud's theory of the Oedipus complex was perhaps another attempt to identify the love that exists, in Fichte's terms, as a man exists, so whole and complete that nothing could or need be added to it. This is a love that denies the existence of woman's love and supports Freud's theory of her as lacking. The contemporary women-centered feminists have suggested a connection between the abstract, universal thinking of Western philosophers and the male sexual organ, whole, single and complete. They see a connection between the male body and the lust for knowledge Fichte described as one "which transcends all experience, which is abstract, absolute, and strictly universal, and which includes within itself beforehand all subsequently possible experience." [92] They also see a connection between this body and a will to make this kind of knowledge real.

In making claims for the speech and writing that can emerge from woman's different body and her different sexuality, the French feminists are saying something akin to Fichte's comments when he associated the child's intimacy with the mother's body and the dangers in mothers' teaching signs and mothers' baby talk. Free from the "pleasure" of the will to knowledge experienced by the man, women can play with signs, even when they play with babies, and they can have dreams of different worlds that do not conform to the world created by men. In this play, they do not respect the mandate that words should be used only to strictly represent the intentions and the truth of the father, or that only the laws of his world or his logic be represented in words. These feminists think that to allow the sight and touch of the mother's body, the sounds of her rhythmic baby talk, and her play with alphabet blocks to become the foundation for the moral education of modern men is humanity's only hope.

5

The Feminine Soul in Henry of Ofterdingen

*All tasted of the divine draught and perceived with
inexpressible joy the friendly greeting of the
Mother within them.*[1]

NOVALIS, *Henry of Ofterdingen*

*What is religion but an infinite harmony, an
eternal unison of loving hearts?*[2]

NOVALIS, *Henry of Ofterdingen*

[*My friend says that the true source of religious
sentiments*] *consists in a peculiar feeling, which
he himself is never without, which he finds
confirmed by many others, and which he may
suppose is present in millions of people. It is a
feeling which he would like to call a sensation
of 'eternity', a feeling as of something limitless,
unbounded—as it were, 'oceanic'. . . . I cannot
discover this "oceanic" feeling in myself.*[3]

FREUD, *Civilization and Its Discontents*

THE SIGHT AND TOUCH of woman's body, not only as mother but also as lover, is the foundation for moral and religious education in the tale *Henry of Ofterdingen*. This story was written by Friedrich von Hardenberg, better known by his pen name Novalis, in 1800. Along with Friedrich von Schlegel, the writer and literary critic, and Friedrich Schleiermacher, the theologian, Novalis founded German romanticism. The language of all nineteenth-century European and American romanticism was influenced by these three Germans, and it was romanticism's images of the feminine soul that Sheila Rowbotham tells us contributed more than any other to the production of "a crop of egg-faced ringleted bonneted fragile girls." [4] But as Rowbotham also points out, in its earliest phase the language of the romantics was a rebellious, even a revolutionary, language. It emerged as a reaction to the mechanical nature of Enlightenment thought and the dehumanizing tendencies of its early technological practice in capitalism. Novalis set out to combat what he thought was the Philistinism of a culture oriented to order and the accumulation of material possessions. In his view, the religion of these Philistines served as their opiate. This religion allowed its believers to feel both secure and moral by encouraging them to project their egos and possessions into a heaven of personal immortality. For Novalis, even the philosophers of freedom's model of the autonomous ego contributed to this false religion. This included Kant's model, with its promotion of the rational illusion of the immortality of the soul. To engender true freedom, to take the opiate of religion away, Novalis sought to create a new religion, a religion of the mother-lover. *Henry of Ofterdingen* is its poetic manifesto.

Like the other work of this early romantic circle, *Henry* was written in the company of women. It was generated in the context of a salon where educated upper- and middle-class men and women, on somewhat equal terms, shared their writing and their feelings about their writing. In this particular salon, feelings got a bit out of hand—most notoriously in Friedrich von Schlegel's affair with the married woman Dorothea Veit, who was the daughter of the Jewish philosopher Moses Mendelssohn. Schlegel described this affair, in what was for the early nineteenth century graphic terms, in his novel *Lucinde*. Because of a scene in which the lovers exchange roles in lovemaking, a scene in which the woman takes the active part and the man luxuriates in passivity, this novel was considered pornographic. The early romantics' behavior and writings earned them the reputation of defending free love and, perhaps even worse, confusing gender identities. Fichte, who had at one time been a participant in this salon, left it because of its immorality.

Of the three fathers of German romanticism, only the theologian Schleiermacher would go on to become a member of the German Protestant establishment. Novalis died not long after writing *Henry*. Schlegel converted to Catholicism and moved to Austria, the largest German Catholic state. But Schleiermacher became a noted official of the Prussian government and, along with Fichte, helped promote a state educational system. Again with Fichte, he founded the University of Berlin, where he did the work that earned him the status of the father of modern liberal Protestant theology. And like Fichte, he was an admirer of Pestalozzi and used his model of education in his theory of religious education. In his famous and lifelong defense of the cultural importance of religion, Schleiermacher espoused a version of the religion of feeling Pestalozzi described as superior to the religion of the mind. And like both Pestalozzi and Novalis, he described this religion as intimately related to women. Nonetheless, it is this father of modern liberal Protestant theology who, in a sense, suppressed Novalis's religion of the mother-lover by domesticating it. Although Schleiermacher appreciated the religious qualities of the feminine soul, he did not share Novalis's visions of a female deity and the new order of her realm.

Henry of Ofterdingen is the story of a male's discov-

ery of self, of his moral development. It takes place on a
journey, which is typical of German *Bildung* narratives.
In this case the journey is through medieval Germany.[5]
At the beginning of his journey, the twenty-year-old man
knows one thing. He is not destined to take up his father's profession as a mechanic or his Philistine life style.
No, Henry is to learn to take free flights of thought and
he needs "only to choose what branch of knowledge [he]
prefers." [6] We learn right away that Henry's free flights
of thought tend to be free flights of the imagination rather
than those described by Fichte.

The story begins in Henry's bedroom in his parents'
home and it ends, after fantastic adventures, in the same
home, with Henry still asking questions about his ego.
Novalis never finished *Henry*. It was left to his friends in
the romantic circle to finish it for him and, in the process,
to try to suppress the tale's powerful mythic vision of the
female god.

The Narrative of Henry
of Ofterdingen

In the first scene, Henry has a pleasurable dream of finding a blue flower. After dreaming of many adventures
that take him through death to resurrection, Henry finds
a pool of water in a mountain cavern in which he im-
merses himself naked. After swimming in ecstasy, he
emerges to sit "on the soft turf by the margin of a fountain, whose waters flowed into the air, and seemed to van-
ish in it. Dark blue rocks with various colored veins rode
in the distance. The daylight around him was milder and
clearer than usual; the sky was of a sombre blue, and
free from clouds. But what most attracted his notice was
a tall, light-blue flower, which stood nearest the fountain,
and touched it with its broad glossy leaves. . . . The flower
bent towards him, and revealed among its leaves a blue,
outspread collar, within which hovered a tender face." [7]

At this point in the dream, Henry's mother awakens him for breakfast.

Henry's father, up early and working industriously, castigates his son for his dreamy late sleep. In one of the constant time warps in this tale, this medieval father gives his son a lecture on the correctness of rational religion. He says, "Dreams are froth.... The times when heavenly visions were seen in dreams have long passed by, nor can we understand the state of mind, which those chosen men, of whom the Bible speaks, enjoyed. Dreams as well as human afIairs must have been of a different nature then. In the age in which we live, there is no direct intercourse with heaven.... The Holy Ghost now speaks to us immediately through the understandings of wise and sensible men, and by the lives and fate of those most distinguished for their piety." [8]

Henry's father has a strange view of God; to a medieval man, God would have been most likely the Creator and providential father and the absolute, arbitrary sovereign of history represented in biblical stories. Henry's father seems to see God in a thoroughly "enlightened" way, as a partner with man in a natural contract whose rules can and ought to be appropriated by man's moral reason and as one who will reward those men for their goodness in a heaven of immortality.

Henry refuses to accept the validity of his father's rational religion. Seeming at first to return us to his own time in the Middle Ages but then propelling us into a Freudian future, he asks his father, "Is not every dream, even the most confused, a peculiar vision, which, though we do not call it sent from heaven, yet makes an important rent in the mysterious curtain, which, with a thousand folds, hides our inward nature from our view?" [9]

Going behind the veil in dreams, Henry tells his father, breaks "up the monotony and even the tenor of our life, to serve as a recreation to the chained fancy. [These dreams] mingle together all the scenes and fancies of life, and change the continual earnestness of age, into the merry sports of childhood." The opiatelike stupor of the father's everyday life and of his rational religion is counterposed by the son to the awakening and energizing potential of dreams. "I am sure that the dream, which I have had this night, has been no profitless occurrence in my life; for I feel that it has, like some vast wheel, caught hold of my soul, and is hurrying me along with it in its mighty revolutions." [10]

Henry's father represents Novalis's Philistine, the one who has been dulled by the opiate of order in life and religion. Nonetheless, even this industrious father is capable of recovering the memory of a time when he was "another sort of man." He tells his wife that his son's dream is because "Henry cannot deny the hour of his conception," an hour full of wine, music, and mutually spirited and ardent sexual passion of the bride and groom.[11] His wife then reminds him that when he was on his journey of self-discovery as a youth, he had his own dream of the blue flower. Protesting that his dream, in contrast to Henry's, was "clear and regular," he explains that it referred to real and familiar experiences in his life. As if to prove it, he retells his dream about a blue flower.[12]

The two men's dreams of the blue flower frame a typical, pleasant domestic scene, breakfast in an industrious household. Immediately, one wonders, Who is right, the father or the son? Do dreams of the blue flower clearly and plainly refer to what is not strange, to what in the father's interpretation is the sign of his natural attraction to a woman with "agreeable and amiable traits of character," whom he had known before he had the dream? [13] Or do dreams of the blue flower initiate revolutions of souls and societies?

Henry, like his father, will find what is not strange, the love of a woman, the noblewoman Matilda, through his dreams of the blue flower. In wooing her he defines the true meaning of religion: "What is religion but an infinite harmony, an eternal unison of loving hearts?

Where two are gathered together, He is indeed among them. Thou wilt be my breath eternally. My bosom will never cease to draw thee to itself. Thou, Matilda, art divine majesty, eternal life in the loveliest of forms. . . . [Your form, your body] is a fragment of the unknown holy world." [14]

Will it be, then, that Henry's dreams of the blue flower, like his father's, merely admit the legitimacy of an early passion, an element of eros, into the housefather's realm of agape? Or are they such a transgression of self-constraint that they free the chained imagination and alter the order of everyday life? Henry's journey of self-discovery holds the answer.

THE JOURNEY AWAY FROM THE FATHER

To learn to take free flights of thought, as Fichte proposed, Henry must leave home, but of all things he takes his mother with him. In fact, his journey of self-discovery is a journey to the homeland of his mother, and the home he leaves is that of his father. Henry is sad to leave "his father and his birthplace. He now experienced for the first time what separation was." [15] This first separation will remain "like the first announcement of death, never to be forgotten." But it is made easier because his mother goes with him. "The world he was leaving did not appear entirely lost, and he embraced [his mother] with redoubled fondness." [16]

From this point on, there is no clear narrative in *Henry.* Henry does take a geographical trip from his father's home in north Germany to his mother's home in south Germany. But this physical journey through time and space provides only the barest of supports for what becomes a series of tales within tales within tales. Time after time a moment in a journey through an identifiable landscape dissolves into another space and time, almost always a space beneath the earth and a past or future time. The reader is forced to accept the sense of being lost in order to experience with Henry the pleasure of visions in which nothing stands still and no identities remain stable. In my narration, the tale has been made much clearer than it is in the text.

The only real supports for the "narrative" are tales, tales told to Henry and two great religious tales. The two religious tales are, first, the familiar Christian story of the birth, death, and resurrection of Christ and, second, the Egyptian tale of the death and resurrection of Osiris. In the latter story, Osiris, the brother and husband of Isis, is murdered twice by jealous gods and resurrected twice by Isis. First, she recovers his body, which has been thrown into a coffin in the sea. Second, she gathers together his dismembered body. She finds all its parts except his penis, which has been thrown again into the sea. To restore his full form, she fashions a penis for him from the earth. In her active mourning for her brother-lover, Isis dons a veil. But even these mythic supports are not secure because their plots and the identities of their characters, like those in the other tales, are continually changing.

Only one thing remains certain. Henry is making progress in his moral development and in his quest for a vocation. It becomes clear almost immediately that Henry is not destined to become a member of the clergy, one of the professions of his day in which he could have been free from the cares of immediate existence to take free flights of thought. But the clergy, the order in medieval society in which all learning had been placed and where it had remained to Novalis's day, fare no better in *Henry* than they did in the tales of Gertrude's soul. Men of the church are "separated from worldly life." These "unsocial and really inexperienced men" give poor counsel to rulers especially because their thoughts "cannot be applied to everyday concerns." [17]

Henry is not willing to accept the role of any thinker who has no direct effect on everyday life. He thinks that there are "two ways by which to arrive at a knowledge of the history of man; the one laborious and boundless, the way of experience; the other apparently but one leap, the way of internal reflection. The wanderer of the first must find out one thing from another by wearisome reckoning; the wanderer of the second perceives the nature of everything and every occurrence directly by their very essence." [18] For Henry, a true thinker, the second path of internal reflection will be the way to truth. But in choosing this path, which was the one approved by Fichte, Henry is stimulated to imagine something quite different from those universal and necessary categories of thought and cultural creation the philosopher thought all men would imagine. He imagines the blue flower, which is woman.

Henry finds dreaming of the blue flower and producing visions of new worlds so pleasurable that he is moved to make these visions real, just as Fichte believed that reflecting on self-reflection and producing ideal prototypes was so pleasurable that men would act to make them real. But the visions induced by dreams of the blue flower do not represent or create a society of law and order. They are wild, confused, apocalyptic visions with no fixed forms, visions in which forms are so fluid that no identities are stable, and we can only guess at this point at the type of society they would lead to. All we know is that the dream of the blue flower, "like some vast wheel," can catch hold of the soul and hurry it "along with it in its mighty revolutions." [19] To understand Henry's moral development and the society for which it prepares him, we must entertain fairly tales and dreams.

THE TALE OF THE UNMARRIED MOTHER

On his journey with his mother, Henry is also accompanied by several merchants who tell Henry a tale about an ancient king. This king, like God the father in the Christian kingdom, is a single parent. In this case his only child is a daughter and his kingdom is endangered, not by sin, but by his daughter's potential infertility.

The future health of this kingdom depends on the "marriage of the blooming princess," but the king's pride in his relation to "superhuman beings, who formerly ruled the world," stands in the way of her acceptance of a suitor.[20] Although the king is related to the gods through his deceased wife, he "had almost unconsciously imbibed a feeling of lofty superiority, which rendered every thought of a connexion of his daughter with a man of lower rank and more obscure origin unendurable."[21]

Despite his status consciousness, the "strict and stern" king has two redeeming qualities that account for the joy and "splendor of his court."[22] One is his love for his daughter, a love that is an extension of his love for his wife, for whom in a reversal of Gertrude's role, he had tried "to create . . . a heaven upon earth."[23] The second is his "passion" for poetry, presumably an ability to dream of the blue flower.[24] These two inclinations came together in the soul of his daughter, who seems to be "the beautiful and embodied spirit of [poetry], conspiring with its magic language."[25] The bodies of women and the magic of language will be interrelated not only in this tale but in all the rest.

The action revolves around the king's loss of his daughter from his kingdom and her return. Wandering in the woods outside her pleasure garden one day, the princess meets an old man and his son, who have been living close to and communing with nature outside the walls of the kingdom. This single parent has educated his son in a Rousseaulike fashion to be a scholar of nature and thus he has never felt the need to introduce him to society. Upon seeing the princess, the son-scholar falls immediately in love, confounded by what he has never seen before, the "enchanting appearance of a majestic female form, which seemed almost immortal, adorned as it was by all the charms of youth and beauty, and by that indescribable fascinating transparency, revealing the tender, innocent, and noble soul."[26] The princess's body both mirrors her feminine soul and incarnates magic language.

During her frequent visits to their cabin, the princess and the son-scholar play the lute and talk of the mysteries of nature. As a result of her communion with the son, she feels as if "a magical veil was spread in wide folds over her clear consciousness. It seemed to her that, when it should be withdrawn, she would find herself in a more spiritual world than this." [27] Her way to this more spiritual world will be through her body.

One day she and the son are caught in a storm while walking in the woods and they take refuge in a cave. Leading her safely inside, the son builds a fire and plays for her on his lute. Then "the innocence of their hearts, the magic harmony of their minds, the united irresistible power of their sweet passion, and their youth, soon made them forget the world and their relations to it, and lulled them, under the bridal song of the tempest and the nuptial torches of the lightning, into the sweetest intoxication by which a mortal couple ever has been blessed. The break of the light blue morning was to them the awakening of a new, blissful world." [28]

Knowing that in this rapturous intercourse she has conceived a child, the princess realizes that she cannot go home. Although she is consoled by her lover's assurance of the holiness of their act, by the "faith" it inspired, and by her images of the child she will have, she worries about her father's reaction.[29] For a year, during which the king longs for his daughter, she is kept hidden in the naturalists' cabin.

One day her lover appears as a poet at a festival in the kingdom and sings the tale of their love for the entertainment of the king. During his song, "an old man with a veiled female of noble stature, carrying in her arms a child of wondrous beauty, who playfully eyed the assembly, and smilingly outstretched its little hands after the diadem of the king, made their appearance." At this moment, the king's eagle "flew down from the tops of the trees with a golden headband...and hovered over the head of the [lover], so that the band fastened around his tresses." [30] Then the lover-father

handed the band to the child, finished his song, and
lifted the veil of the princess.

In one brief scene, images of Isis, the Virgin Mary
with the Christ Child, the babe Christ claiming the
power of God the father, the baptism of Christ, and
the wedding headband of virginity swirl together. It is
no wonder that with all this revelation, the king experiences "nothing but joy." He embraces his daughter and
her lover, and "taking the child, the king raised it
towards Heaven." Then "the night became a sacred
festive eve of promise" and life "henceforth was but one
delightful jubilee." [31]

In this tale the health of the kingdom is saved by
the passion of the princess. Through her transgression,
the king is led to realize that "it is not the crown or the
kingdom that makes the king." The kingdom of the
father is fulfilled by the sexual act and fertility of his
daughter, and the last vestiges of his sternness are wiped
away by his realization that "it is the full, overflowing
feeling of happiness . . . the consciousness of perfect satisfaction and content" that makes a man a king.[32]

Here the sacralization of the domestic sphere and
the centrality of the mother takes a shape different from
that proposed by Pestalozzi. Whereas Pestalozzi found
innate order and society-saving love in Gertrude's feminine soul, Novalis presents sexuality, the eros, of woman
and her act of giving birth as the guarantee of the health
of the kingdom.

THE TEMPTATION TO JOIN THE ARMY

The tale of the princess is followed by one that appears
to offer a sharp contrast. As might be expected on any
medieval male's journey of self-discovery, Henry meets
Christian knights of the Crusades. Initially stirred by
their tales of their mission, he begins to be deflected from
his quest for an intellectual vocation and imagines that
taking up the sword in defense of the cross and holy
sepulcher of Christ would be the height of heroic de-

votion, a fulfillment of the male religious soul. As his
enthusiasm grows during a drinking bout with the bois-
terous knights who are preparing for the distant battle,
he is further enticed into joining them by their promise
that if he guides his "sword skillfully, beauteous captives shall not be wanting." [33]

The placement of this tale after that of the passionate princess suggests that we are being warned of
the "seductions" of soldiers. But in this tale the seductions are legitimate; indeed, rape seems almost to be
blessed by the Holy Virgin. The knights sing, "We soon
shall drench in joyous mood the sacred grave with hea-
then blood" under the aegis of the Holy Virgin.[34]

The knights' song of blood and the Holy Virgin puts
"Henry's whole soul . . . in commotion. The tomb rose
before him like a youthful form, pale and stately, upon
a massive stone in the midst of a savage multitude,
cruelly maltreated, and gazing with sad countenance
upon a cross, which shone in the background with vivid
outlines, and multiplied itself in the tossing waves of
the ocean." [35] But just as Henry is about to be carried
away with a warrior's devotion to saving Christ's tomb,
his mother intervenes. She calls him away from the
knights to meet the lady of the castle. After greeting
her, Henry is lured into a walk by the beauty outdoors
and he does not return to the company of the knights.
As the approaching evening's beauty begins to "soothe"
his soul, he hears "a female voice accompanied by won-
derful music played on a lute." [36]

The voice Henry hears is that of one of the knights'
"beauteous captives," a Saracen woman singing of her
plight of exile. Henry comes upon her as she cradles her
child "ten or twelve years old" in her arms.[37] This image
of the sorrowful unmarried mother from Jerusalem lost
with her child replaces that of the bloodthirsty Virgin
of the knights' song. Moreover, the woman, Zulima, tells
Henry her own tale of Christ's tomb. She praises the
goodness of her people and of the "romantic beauties of

the fertile regions of Arabia, which lay like happy is-
lands in the midst of impassable, sandy wastes, refuge
places for the oppressed and weary, like colonies of
Paradise." [38] She pleads, "Believe not what you are told
of the cruelties of my countrymen." [39] If their kindness
and humanity were respected by the Christians, "how
beautifully might [Christ's] sacred tomb become the cradle of a happy union, the source of an alliance blessing
all forever!" [40]

Henry believes her version of the tale of the tomb
of Christ. After hearing it, his "warlike inspiration had
entirely vanished." [41] Then Zulima, Henry, and the child
walk back to the castle, he, like the princess's lover, with
lute in hand.

As Henry begins his journey the next day, he and
Zulima exchange gifts. She gives him a golden headband,
ornamented with the "strange characters" of her name
in her mother tongue. Henry gives her a veil.[42] Another
unmarried mother goddess leads Henry on to his salvation of self-discovery.

THE TOMB OF CHRIST AND THE WOMB
OF EARTH

With Henry's next adventure, the reinterpretation of the
cross and tomb of Christ is complete. The historical and
geographical significance of the tomb for Christianity
was brought into question by Zulima's talk of her people and motherland. Now the cave-sepulcher becomes
a mine, a tunnel down into the earth itself, and its
sacred contents become the secrets of mother earth.
Henry is taken down into the mine, where he is given a
lamp and a wooden cross to guide his way. Deep in the
bosom of the earth, he learns the secrets of metallurgy.
His guide tells Henry that after he had learned them
himself for the first time, he gazed on the crucifix and
"clearly understood the holy meaning of this mysterious image." [43]

Henry learns that the discovery of the mysteries of

precious metals carried in the bosom of the earth places the miner in a special and holy relationship with nature, a relationship through which he can recognize "the interior essence, and the manifold, primitive energies of things." In contrast to society's desire to possess material things the miner knows the truth—that nature "will never be the possession of any single individual. In the form of property it becomes a terrible poison, which destroys rest, excites the ruinous desire of drawing everything within the reach of its possessor, and carries with it a train of wild passions and sorrows." [44] The miner has a different relationship to nature, that of a bridegroom to a bride in a marriage in which the bride is not a possession, not the object of wild passions. And the joy of discovering the mysteries of nature is like the joy of sexual intercourse in such a marriage. Moreover, for the miner, his most prized discovery is the vein that contains precious metal, called *Mutter*, "mother" or "mother's blood." [45]

Henry speculates that miners are "inverted astrologers": for astrologers, the "higher world [the sky] is a book of futurity." For miners, "the earth is a memorial of the primeval world." [46] Their truth lies not in the light of heaven but in a space deep in the bosom of the earth, deep in the primeval and chaotic material of its origins.

IN HIS MOTHER'S HOMELAND: THE TALE OF FABLE

When Henry finally reaches his mother's homeland in the joyous south of Germany, his branch of knowledge becomes clear. He is to be a poet. His grandfather, recognizing this, introduces Henry to the poet of his kingdom, the nobleman Klingsohr, whose daughter is the beautiful Matilda. When Henry meets Matilda, he wonders, "Do I not feel as I felt in that dream about the blue flower? What peculiar connection is there between Matilda and that flower? That face, which bowed to-

wards me from the petals, was Matilda's heavenly countenance. . . . She will dissolve me into music. She will
become my inmost soul, the guardian of my holy fire." [47]

Matilda never becomes the guardian of Henry's home
fire in the same way that his mother became the guardian
of his father's. He dreams of her death and at the end
of the book we find him at home again, mourning her
loss and questioning a wise man about his ego.

In the last tale of *Henry* which is told by Klingsohr,
it becomes clear why dreams of the blue flower do not
signify domestic bliss in a housefather's home. For Klingsohr's tale is the revelation of the religion of the goddess. Through a series of ever-changing scenes and identities, the frozen kingdom of the father virtually explodes
through a constant fluidity of forms into the realm of the
mother.[48]

The tale of Fable begins with a scene of an old hero-
warrior wandering in the frozen kingdom of Arcturus.
In the city of the kingdom, there is perfect "symmetry"
and "noble," classic style.[49] Light reflects brilliantly off
the walls, all frozen in order. It is the beautiful, but
static, kingdom of the father. Stasis and the cycle of eternal return belong to this well-ordered realm in which
peace is encircled by the instruments of war, and the
hero-warrior, not mothers, ensures that things do not
change.

As he enters the palace of King Arcturus, the hero-
warrior finds Freya, the beautiful princess, lounging sen-
suously on her throne of sulfur. Freya indicates that the
hero's quests have been in vain by asking him, "Have
you discovered nothing yet?" Inside the palace the soft
light illumining everything emanates from the hands of
the maidens who were massaging the body of the princess, "which seemed to be blended of milk and crim-
son." [50] Freya seems to want to take on the instruction
of the hero when she asks to touch his shield. But instead she "grasped his hand, pressed it tenderly to her
heavenly bosom, and touched his shield. His armor rang,

and a pervasive force animated his entire body.[51] But before our hero can learn his lesson, the king enters. A beautiful bird above his throne anounces the king's arrival and sings to him about love and desire.[52]

As in this opening scene woman's physical desire throughout this tale initiates the quest for salvation of the frozen kingdom and for man's self-discovery. The hero's awakening by and to a woman's physical desire will result in a peace free of the instruments of war. Here the salvific fulfillment of desire in a mutually satisfying heterosexual intercourse will entail the recovery of a sleeping queen. In a reversal of the Demeter-Persephone myth, this recovery is achieved by the daughter's, Fable's, liberation of the lost mother.

The effective quest for the true kingdom begins when the king, after consulting a version of tarot cards, commands the hero, whom he identifies as Iron, to throw his sword "into the world so that they may learn where Peace is resting." The sword flies into the distant mountain range and bursts into sparks.[53]

The Nursery of Eden. With this burst of fire, the scene of the tale shifts to a new part of the kingdom—the nursery of the babe Eros. Here Eros is attended by his wet nurse, Ginnistan, who is also caring for his foster sister Fable, the heroine of the tale. The villain, a busy scribe, is writing by the bright light of a lamp and looking sullenly at the children and their nurse. Ginnistan shields the babe Eros from the scribe's light with her colorful veil.

King Arcturus, the father of the children, enters and leaves the nursery repeatedly. When he enters, he always dictates to the scribe, who records his words faithfully. But this father's wisdom in the scribe's hand is subject to the judgment of another character in the nursery, a "noble, godlike woman who stood leaning against an altar on which there stood a dark basin with clear water, which she gazed into with a serene smile." [54]

This woman is Sophia. The scribe must hand his pages
of dictation to Sophia to be dipped into the basin before the words on the page will become permanent and
before they can be put into a great book. The liquid in
the basin determines which, if any, of the father's words
remain on the pages. Sometimes, to the consternation of
the scribe, the words are erased. Could the magic power
of Sophia's liquid to erase the words of the father be
what Fichte feared?

Throughout this tale, Sophia's liquid is the saving
sacrament of the kingdom. Even in this early scene its
magic qualities dominate. Only later will we learn what
it is. At times Sophia sprinkles drops of the liquid on
the nurse and the children, like holy water. When it
touches them, it "dissolves into a blue mist that produces a thousand strange images, constantly flowing
around them and changing shape." But when one of the
drops happens to touch the scribe, it changes into fixed
forms, geometrical shapes, which he carefully strings on
a thread and hangs around his "scrawny neck." [55]

There is a "real" mother in this scene. Like the
father, she enters and leaves the nursery repeatedly, always carrying a domestic utensil, a habit that deeply
disturbs the scribe. Although the mother sometimes
nurses Fable, she is often too busy. Thus it is Ginnistan
who gives nourishment and love to the child.

All of a sudden the father brings into the nursery
a sliver of iron he has found outdoors, a piece of Iron's
shattered sword, and it proves to be the spark that ignites
desire in the nursery. But, first, in a last futile attempt
to keep order in the nursery, the scribe takes the sliver
of iron, suspends it from a string, and discovers its usefulness: It is a compass. The scribe, like a true scientist,
immediately writes a long report on his discovery. But
when Sophia dips the paper containing this report in
the bowl of water, it comes out blank.

Next Ginnistan takes the iron and bends it into the
shape of an uroboros, a serpent biting its tail. Now we

we have the serpent in the garden, and like Eve, Ginnistan plays with it. In her play she awakens the sleeping Eros, who grabs the serpent and, surprisingly, jumps, completely naked, from his cradle. Energized by the toy, he begins to grow. He then asks Sophia's permission to drink from the bowl, and as he drinks the liquid is replenished and Eros miraculously grows to the full form of a man. Finished with his drinking and growth, Eros asks Ginnistan for her veil to cover his genitals.

Ginnistan gives Eros her veil, but it is too late. Desire has invaded the nursery—Ginnistan's desire. She takes "infinite pleasure" in Eros and "clasp[s] him to her with the fervor of a bride" [56] Two acts interrupt her seduction. First, Sophia checks her by pointing to the serpent. Just then, the "real" mother enters and Eros leaves Ginnistan to go to her. But still all is not well. In fact, fully aware that things are getting out of hand in the nursery, the scribe leaves angrily. The father enters and, seeing his wife and son hugging, he approaches Ginnistan. After Sophia also leaves, though less angry than the scribe, the king willingly satisfies the nurse's desire in an adjoining chamber.[57] During all this shifting of desire, Fable, who has stolen the scribe's pen, records it all.

For a moment, it seems that all will return to normal. Sophia and the scribe return. The father and a happy Ginnistan reenter and return to their work places.[58] And the scribe tries desperately to restore order. Furious at Fable, he asks Sophia to clean with her liquid the paper on which Fable has written. But Fable's writing emerges from the bowl unchanged.

As in *Leonard and Gertrude,* it is the mother, the real, domestic mother, who succeeds in restoring order, not the scribe. She breast-feeds Fable and, like Gertrude in Hubel-Rudy's house, cleans the room, opens the windows, and prepares food for a feast. The father remains at his business, and his passion for Ginnistan is thus constrained by distance. Finally, Eros begins to act like a proper son and gets ready to join the army. Putting on a suit of armor, he prepares himself for a journey-battle to prove his manhood. All might yet have been well—the domestic mother might have succeeded like Gertrude in restoring order—but Eros rejects the scribe's "detailed itinerary" and asks Sophia to guide his journey.[59]

It does not take long to realize that this godlike woman's wisdom will supersede that of the domestic mother. First, Sophia designates Ginnistan as Eros's travel guide. But to keep her from "lead[ing him] into temptation," she has Ginnistan exchange external forms with the mother—a strategy that is sure to fail. As if to compensate for this, she gives the pair vials of liquid from her bowl to take with them. Yet her plan for Eros's journey to manhood brings temporary happiness. The father is thrilled because the exchange of the women's forms legitimates his desire for Ginnistan, who is now the outer form of his wife. Even the scribe is happy, but only because Eros and Ginnistan are leaving the nursery. He wishes they would take Fable with them. Only the real domestic mother is "distressed" at her son's separation from her. At the parting, the father is absent, unconcerned.[60]

The Dream of the Blue Flower. The journey of Eros becomes immediately the journey of his lover-mother Ginnistan back to her father's, the Moon's, kingdom. The serpent-compass guides this lost daughter back to a father who has been yearning for his daughter.

In the joy of his reunion with his daughter, whose true identity he recognizes from her voice, the Moon king grants Eros access to his treasure palace, a place of visions. Entering with Ginnistan, Eros has a vision of the time when the earth was flooded, when an apocalyptic battle between life and death took place. It is hard to imagine even Hubel-Rudy's wife having a wilder vision than the one Eros has. At first he sees peaceful scenes of cities, castles, fertile fields, and mountain sheep in the many colors of the rainbow. But soon the horizons of

his vision begin to expand and in the distance appear
scenes of horror—a shipwreck, an earthquake, a battle.
In the foreground appear vignettes of peace—the joyful
meal of peasant people, a loving couple caressing each
other. Then the horizons shift, and in the foreground
appears the corpse of a young man mourned by his lover
and in the background a "lovely mother with her child
on her breast, angels sitting at her feet and gazing from
the branches over her head." Isis and the Virgin Mary.
Suddenly these scenes, like other scenes throughout
Henry, flow "together at last into a mysterious spectacle"
and prepare the way for the vision of the true divinity
and for what is in the blue flower.[61]

At first, "heaven and earth" are in a "complete up-
roar." Death attacks life on every front. "With un-
heard-of atrocities, [an] army of phantoms" tears "the
tender limbs of the living to pieces. A towering funeral
pyre" rises and "amidst the most gruesome howling the
children of Life" are "consumed by the flames." [62]

But then comes salvation: From the ashes there
arises, not a phoenix, but a "milk-blue stream," mother's
milk, to flood the scene of horrors. On top of the saving
liquid floats a "flower of wondrous beauty" and over it
arches a rainbow on which sits Sophia with her bowl. At
her side sits a "lordly man with an oak wreath about his
locks and a palm of peace in his right hand instead of a
scepter." [63] The rainbow throne of the goddess Sophia and
her consort arches over the flower, and the vision of this
revelation is complete: "A lily leaf [bends] over the chalice of the floating flower, and upon it [sits] little Fable,
singing the sweetest songs to the accompaniment of a
harp. In the chalice [lies] Eros himself, [bending] over
a beautiful sleeping maiden who [clings] tightly to him. A
smaller blossom enclose[s] the two of them, so that from
the hips down they [seem] to be transformed into a single
flower." [64] Thus the blue flower is woman's body, woman's sexuality, and woman's desire is the sacrament of the
goddess Sophia's realm.

Eros is in rapture after this vision, but enervated by

it, he is now prey to Ginnistan's seduction. Rather than giving him Sophia's liquid to refresh himself, the mother-lover urges him to take a bath, from which he emerges "intoxicated." Still dreaming of his lover in the flower, he mistakes Ginnistan even in the form of his mother for his lover, gives into his desires, and feels "the most sensuous of pleasures." [65]

Fable's Journey to the Underworld. As though censoring this vision and its aftermath, Novalis abruptly shifts the scene from the moon to the nursery, where, in an attempt to gain control, the scribe has imprisoned the mother and is preparing to kill her by turning the altar into a blazing funeral pyre. Arcturus, the father, is not regarded as a genuine threat and is merely neutralized by being held in captivity, where he is deprived of everything except bread and water.

Fable will save the father's kingdom through her own journey, which takes the form of her descent into an underworld, a world peopled by evil women. Her passageway to this world is under the altar, where she hides from the scribe. Through a door in the floor, Fable descends into the darkness where a sphinx guards the door to the room in which the Fates are spinning the threads of life. To pass, Fable asks the sphinx three questions: Where are my sisters? Where is Love? Where is Sophia? Having found the magic words, *Sophia* and *Love,* to the sphinx's dismay, Fable is allowed to pass.

Immediately the babe Fable meets the doorkeeper of the realm of the Fates, by whose breasts she knows she can be fed. But in contrast to her mother's and Ginnistan's breasts, the doorkeeper's breasts are so full of milk that she cannot rise and the hungry Fable rejects the overfull mother bound to the earth and passes her by. Fable next asks the crones' permission to join them in spinning, but she tells them that she may disturb them because when she spins she must speak. Warning Fable that if she breaks the thread of her work, it will strangle her, the crones give her permission. As she gleefully spins, Fable sings what could have been a song in *How Gertrude Teaches Her Children*. Not dropping any threads, she chants of weaving a unity of hearts so closely into her cloth of life that evil and sorrow can find no place.

The scribe, having found the hidden door, descends and interrupts Fable's song. He plots with the Fates to convince Fable she must leave them to fetch the oil of tarantulas to refill their overturned spinning lamps. He attempts to win their favor by telling them that he intends to release them from the power of the queen-mother whose command has confined them to this sphere to spin the threads of life. Although the Fates cooperate with the scribe, Fable escapes again, this time down a ladder into the dungeon where the father is imprisoned.

Powerless in the bowels of the earth, Arcturus sits on a prison throne that resembles that of Sophia's consort seen in Eros's vision, but this throne is missing the sacrament of the blue flower. The father's head is encircled by a metal band, not a garland, and while he does have a lily in one hand and not a scepter, in his other hand he still holds scales of justice. Moreover, an eagle and a lion, the symbols for biblical evangelists, sit at his feet. To save him, Fable asks for a lyre, and the music transports her over the sea of ice of the father's frozen kingdom to her mother, whom we now understand to be Ginnistan.[66]

Fable hardly recognizes the now pale and worn Ginnistan, and the daughter worries that the mother is too weak to feed her.[67] Nevertheless, Ginnistan takes Fable to the breast, smiling down at her and telling her the consequences of her intercourse with Eros. Ginnistan does not regret satisfying her desire because she has been made immortal. But she confesses that Eros acted like a "heavenly marauder," seeming to want to destroy her, to defeat a "victim." [68] When they awoke from this illicit, violent lovemaking, "long silvery wings had grown over [Eros's] shoulders, covering the enchanting fullness and curves of his figure. The force that had sprung up in him and so suddenly made a young man out of the boy seemed to have withdrawn entirely into the shining wings, and he was once again a boy." [69] Now in willful childishness, Eros flies through the realm, inflicting unfulfilled desire on those he hits with his arrows, and Ginnistan longs to return him to manhood but he will not come to her. It will be Fable, his sister, who will save Eros from his castration and his victims, including Ginnistan, from unfulfilled desire. The wantonness, the madness, of Eros will be constrained, his wings will be clipped, not by the restoration of the order of the father's kingdom or by his powers of judgment, but by the establishment of Sophia's reign.

Before Fable can return to her father's, Arcturus's, kingdom, the scribe murders the queen-mother. Fable sees the flames of her foster mother's funeral pyre from a distance and despairs until she looks to the heaven and sees Sophia's blue veil stretching over the earth. The fire of the mother's death is so strong that it steals the fire of the sun and extinguishes it. Terrified by what his act of murder has brought about, the scribe tries to put out the death flames of the mother but fails. Fable also rushes to the flames, but it is too late.

Once again Fable descends beneath what is now the altar of the mother's sacrifice, through the realm of the Fates to her father, who knows that the flames of his wife's death have melted the ice of his kingdom. But he tells Fable he cannot come out of his dungeon because "alone I am not king." [70] He tells Fable, "Blessed child, you are our liberator." [71]

Fable saves the kingdom by gathering together the ashes of her mother. Presiding at a new altar in what was the nursery, the priestess-goddess Sophia begins to order her realm. In the room now is what seems to be the bier of the father. Like Sleeping Beauty, he must be awakened by a caress, that of Ginnistan, who has now identified her true mate. Eros, whose wings have been clipped by Fable, now lies in his armor at Sophia's feet.[72] Fable presents the urn containing her mother's ashes to Sophia and tells her that she has unlocked the secret of immortality and thus "will be the soul of our lives." [73]

What follows is a rerun of the initial awakening of desire in the nursery, but now the order within which it can be satisfied is established. First, given a gold mirror by Fable, Ginnistan lays her hand on the king's heart and awakens him. "The Father rose up, his eyes flashed, and as beautiful and significant as his figure was, at the same time his body seemed to be an endlessly responsive fluid that revealed every impression in the finest and most varied movements." [74] Sophia then consecrates the union of Ginnistan and the father, instructing them to always consult the gold mirror, which will destroy "every illusion."

Next the goddess pours the mother's ashes into her bowl and passes it to everyone to drink. The mother "was present in each, and her sacred and mysterious presence seemed to transfigure them all." [75] The recipients of this sacrament thus come to know what they had lacked—the capacity to be endlessly responsive to each other. After each has drunk from the bowl, Sophia delivers a sermon: "Out of pain the new world is born, and in tears the ashes are dissolved to become the drink of eternal life. In each one dwells the heavenly Mother, to bear each child eternally. Do you feel the sweet birth in the throbbing of your breast?" Then she pours the rest of the liquid in the bowl onto the altar and the ground trembles.[76]

The order of this new world, which Fable and Eros go out to establish throughout the kingdom, is one of fluid forms held above destructive chaos. It is one in which war is confined to a chess game, a game kept only as a reminder of a troubled time in the frozen kingdom. Above all, it is one of satisfied desire. Now Eros, shedding his armor, recognizes Freya as his true lover and, in a mirror reversal of his mother-lover's awakening of the king, arouses the princess from a deep sleep with a kiss.

In the final scene in the throne room, Freya's bench has become the king's throne. Going to his wedding bed, the king leads his subjects in a love feast. Fable, riding on the prophetic bird, now the phoenix, above the throne, declares, "The Mother is among us; her presence will keep us happy eternally." [77]

After this tale of the divine mother is a fragment of a section entitled "Fulfillment." It describes Henry, now back at home after Matilda's death, discussing the meaning of his visions and experiences with a wise old man. To try, as we will see these two do in the next chapter, to make sense of Henry's visions and especially of Klingsohr's tale is a difficult task. Novalis's shifting images appear to defy sense and order but with probing they reveal important meanings.

6

Domestication of Henry's Visions of the Feminine Soul

*All transformation and assimilation, all procreation
and destruction, comes through the mediation
of fluids—the fluid is the same as the delicate veil
on the raiment of the mother Isis.*[1]

BAADER, *Elements of Physiology*

*Labour is, in the first place, a process in which
both Man and Nature participate, and in which
man of his own accord, starts, regulates, and
controls the material relations between himself
and Nature.*[2]

MARX, *Capital*

*Oh, Mother, you might just as well be the happy
mother of the divine babe! And you are perhaps
sorry that you are not? And is this, do you suppose,
why mothers would rather have boys?*[3]

SCHLEIERMACHER, *Christmas Eve*

Novalis's representation of the feminine soul in *Henry of Ofterdingen* went far beyond that found in Pestalozzi's works on Gertrude's soul. Novalis's images challenged every aspect of the religious and social order accepted by nineteenth-century German men and women. The images of the saving grace of the unmarried mothers, the princess and Zulima, of the revelations waiting deep in the bosom of mother earth, and of a sensuous matriarchy with a ritual of drinking the mother's body are startling. Further, they stand without a final explanation at the end, and it is therefore difficult to state simply the moral of Henry's story of self-development. Novalis may have recognized that he had created in this great tale a story he could not finish—for the simple reason that he did not know how. The formal ending of the story is unsatisfactory and draws attention to the difficulty in articulating and accepting the meaning of the feminine soul envisioned here.

Novalis ends his tale with Henry's return home, where he meets a physician named Sylvester, a wise man who attempts to help Henry understand the meaning of his journey. As he begins to talk to Henry, Sylvester confesses that what most surprises him about his moral education is that his father put it into the hands of his mother and "has carefully abstained from taking any part in your development." [4] For the wise man, this means that Henry has "been permitted to grow up free from all parental restraints." [5] It means that Henry's mother did not discipline him as his father would have. But Henry, now forlorn and mourning for Matilda, is uncertain that he has taken a superior path of moral development. He defends his father by insisting that his father did contribute to his education and that he now has a new appreciation for his fatherland. Nonetheless, he asks, "But must the mother die, that the children may thrive? Does the father remain sitting alone at [her] tomb, in tears forever?" [6] Remembering the dreams of the blue flower, he asks, "When will there be no more terror or pain, want or evil in the universe?" [7]

Sylvester, who now begins to sound suspiciously like Fichte, answers, "When there is but one power, the power of conscience; when nature becomes chaste and pure. There is but one cause of evil—common frailty—and this frailty is nothing but a weak moral susceptibility, and a deficiency in the attraction of freedom." [8] The wise man insists that "there is but one virtue—the pure, solemn Will," which exercises its mastery over things and takes the place of "God on earth." [9] Apparently won over, Henry exclaims, "Thus the true spirit of Fable is the spirit of virtue in friendly disguise." [10]

Just after this, the text stops. Neither Henry nor the wise man gets a chance to explain how the tale of Fable can be allegorized as a tale of conscience. Novalis's friend, the poet Ludwig Tieck, who edited his works after his death, filled in briefly what he thought would have been the rest of *Henry,* but he knew that what we really have is what Novalis left us—a fragmented, open-ended piece. Tieck wrote, "Perhaps many a reader will be grieved at the fragmentary character of these verses and words, as well as myself, who would not regard with any more devout sadness a piece of some ruined picture of Raphael or Correggio," the artists of glorious images of the Virgin Mary.[11]

The image of the Virgin Mary was, without a doubt, ruined in the tales of *Henry,* and any attempt to subordinate the images of woman to God's word and man's conscience will entail changing those images. One of Novalis's friends, Schleiermacher, did attempt this task and thereby suppressed the religious qualities of Novalis's representation of the feminine soul. Like Fichte responding to Pestalozzi, Schleiermacher responding to Novalis's work rejected the notion of the feminine soul because of its threat to the male-defined, established order. Before looking at this suppression we need to try to describe the feminine soul in Novalis's work.

Novalis's Image of the Feminine Soul

In *Henry* and in Pestalozzi's *How Gertrude Teaches Her Children*, the feminine soul is a psychobiological essence, extending on one side to the divine and, on the other, to the female body. On the divine side it becomes the Virgin Mary, Isis, Sophia, Aphrodite, Demeter, and then an unrecognizable God the mother—a ruined Correggio. But, in *Henry*, when it reaches into the female body, in a sense it goes beyond the nurturing, loving maternal body to which Pestalozzi attached it and reaches to female sexual desire. Because of this extension of the feminine soul, the spirit of Fable is far more than a friendly disguise for virtue understood as the pure will that can create brotherly love. Just what the tale of *Henry* does mean is impossible to state in ordinary terms. It so overstimulates the imagination that the mind cannot hold the images and scenes long enough to interpret them. Novalis's images and narrative are truly disorienting in a way in which Pestalozzi's expressions about God the mother, despite Fichte's inability to understand them, are not.

Since we cannot state clearly the meaning of *Henry* by analyzing its images, we must approach the question of interpretation from another perspective. The opening of *Henry* suggests the plot of a housefather book. If we compare the plot of *Henry* with the pattern of household relations described by the housefather books, we can more easily grasp Novalis's vision. In comparing the two works, *Henry* and the typical housefather book, we see at once that in the tale of Fable eros is never replaced by the agape of the housefather's realm. In *Henry* the father's will is always powerless in the face of Eros, who is born from a woman, rendered wild through a woman, and tamed by a woman. But when the violence of Eros is checked, it is not turned into the pleasure of the will to truth and to power that produces brotherly love. Eros is tamed into erotic satisfaction.

The dangers of woman's desire lurk at the center of this plot even as they lurk in the implicit plot of the old housefather story. The intercourse of Eros and Ginnistan is violent. The mother-lover is victimized and the son-lover is castrated. Unfulfilled desire is born and spread abroad. But in this story evil is overcome by the daughter, Fable, who recovers the victimized mother's body and with it institutes the sacrament of the kingdom.

At the end of this tale, Eve-Ginnistan does not lose her desire in submission and obedience to her husband. Her desire is satisfied by the king, whose body after being awakened by her touch "seemed to be an endlessly responsive fluid." [12] Even in the beginning of the tale, even in the nursery of Eden, Eve-Ginnistan's desire is satisfied. In this story, women make, play with, control, and ultimately enjoy the power of the serpent.

When we look further we find that Eve-Ginnistan's, the mother-lover's, desire is not siphoned off by the pains of childbirth. Remarkably, this tale saturated with the mother and mother's milk lacks any image of pregnancy. The only fruits of sexual intercourse described are those of Eros and Ginnistan's lovemaking, a virtual litter of little cupids, who join the boy Eros in his willful planting of unfulfilled desire. But descriptions of the pregnant woman are missing. Here the lover is always already a mother. Birth is there from the beginning.

Participation in the sacramental religion of this realm of woman's desire, by drinking a mixture containing the ashes of the mother's body, transforms both the souls and bodies of its adherents. First, it makes "sweet birth" a quality of all souls. Each believer, male and female, is to "bear each child eternally." [13] Second, the recipients of the sacrament of the mother's body come to know what they lack—bodies that can be endlessly responsive to each other. The sight, the touch, the drinking of the mother's body, is the foundation for Henry's moral and religious education. The housefathers of the Reformation and of the nineteenth century could not imagine this and could not allegorize this into a tale of conscience.

THE FLUIDS OF CREATION

In Fable's tale the original transcendent creative act is the act of birth; it is there from the beginning. The premise of creation is not a thinking, willing ego, but physical birth. Novalis, like Fichte and the other philosophers of freedom, believed in an inner, unique source of self-development, but in contrast to them, he saw this source not as free will but as a psychobiological energy. Not as conscience but as the feminine soul. For him, the image of Eros and his lover in the floating flower of Sophia's realm was grounded in what he thought was a scientific physiology. In his numerous reflections on science, Novalis had conjectured that in the beginning of all life and of all individuality in physical nature and humans, there was an *Urmaterial,* a primordial material. This material was not merely the passive stuff from which a spiritual principle of creation, a will, formed the world. Although unformed, it was a "medium of dormant potentials," a "primitive," self-begetting fluid.[14] This original and originating material energy of life could be related to and stimulated by external influences, but it was not reducible to them or completely dependent on them for shaping the individuality of phenomena in physical nature or in human personalities. One of Novalis's biographers explains that this original reproductive fluid was, for Novalis, the feminine principle and it superseded "the purely triggering [and mechanical] function" of the masculine principle.[15] Novalis, he points out, agreed with the philosopher and scientist Baader, who wrote, "All transformation and assimilation, all procreation and destruction, comes through the mediation of fluids—the fluid is the same as the delicate veil on the raiment of the mother Isis."[16]

The implication of this physiology is that the life energy of the womb is boundless. The biological pole of the feminine soul in *Henry* is not a fixed, determining limit on female energy, or merely a nurturing maternal body, but a primal cosmic material source of all transforming potential.

In what could well be a commentary on Novalis's image of sexual union in the blue flower and its scientific physiology, Simone de Beauvoir explained that neither the image nor the science is "normal" for males, for neither reflects their sexuality. In the male sexuality that is accepted in the West as normative, the male "feels a repugnance for the mysterious alchemies of life." [17] It is true that in the sexual act "man embraces the loved one and seeks to lose himself in the infinite mystery of the flesh. But . . . his normal sexuality tends to dissociate Mother from Wife." [18] Yet de Beauvoir recognized that at times men *could* imagine a vision of the blue flower. She wrote:

> And so it is when there flourishes a vitalist romanticism that desires the triumph of Life over Spirit, then the magical fertility of the land, of woman, seems to be more wonderful than the contrived operations of the male; then man dreams of losing himself anew in the maternal shadows that he may find there again the true sources of his being. The mother is the root which, sunk in the depths of the cosmos, can draw up its juices; she is the fountain whence springs forth the living water, water that is also a nourishing milk, a warm spring, and made of earth and water, rich in restorative virtues.[19]

De Beauvoir, like Baader and Novalis, thinks that the image of Isis has historically represented this unusual male science and desire. It is important for us to realize that unlike the more customary representations of the mother in male-dominated societies, woman in the vision of the blue flower does represent culture. She is the root that is sunk in the depths of the cosmos and draws up its juices, and like the mother goddess in *Henry*, she renders fluid a frozen static world.

THE FLUIDITY OF LANGUAGE

For men a vitalist romanticism like that of *Henry* is rare. According to de Beauvoir, men ordinarily associate themselves with infinite spirit, not matter and the body. Men want to be "inevitable, like a Pure Idea, like the One, the All, the absolute Spirit." [20] Luce Irigaray also contrasts a vision of female sexuality similar to Novalis's with a sexuality and a thought focused on the one, the pure idea. In Irigaray's view, woman "experiences pleasure almost everywhere" and thus her sexuality is "much more diversified, more multiple in its differences, more complex, more subtle" than the sexuality normally imagined by men.[21] And this different experience requires a different language to describe it.

Irigaray draws a connection between woman's body and woman's language, a connection that characterizes the theory of women-centered feminists. Woman's different sexuality, if she dares to speak from it, produces a use of language that men find hard to understand. Woman speaks in unfinished sentences and with contradictory words that "seem a little crazy to the logic of reason, [to] a code prepared in advance." [22] Like the code of language that Fichte thought could be prepared in advance for people by scholars expressing men's audible thought, this code defines the meaning of words clearly and insists that an identification between subject and object be made by finishing sentences. When woman speaks from her different sexual pleasure, a pleasure that has no fixed point of identity and no central form, "one must listen to her differently in order to hear an *'other meaning' which is constantly in the process of weaving itself, at the same time ceaselessly embracing words and yet casting them off to avoid becoming fixed, immobilized."* [23] This sort of different use of language produces meaning different from that produced by male systems of thought and the male will to power.

We can see a similar understanding of language at work in *Henry*. Think of Sophia obliterating the father's words, faithfully recorded by the scribe, in the liquid of the sacrament of the mother's body and of Fable's writing of Ginnistan's desire remaining uneffaced. Think of Fable spinning the future of a peaceful and erotically satisfied realm with words drawn from the fluids in her body. And think how confusing and contradictory and fragmentary all of *Henry* is.

In describing his own use of words, Novalis defined poetry as "the art of arbitrarily using the physical world." [24] He declared, "Words become magical when purified and cleansed of their everyday meanings." [25] It is worth trying to understand these statements; through them we can understand the significance of language for women-centered feminists and Fichte's fear of the consequences of mothers' teaching the alphabet to their children.

Although Novalis unequivocally rejected mechanism in any form, he thought that mathematics was a proper model for poetic language. Language, at least the language of poetry, ought to be an arbitrary, human-made system of signs like that of mathematics. Poetic signs ought to be like mathematical signs—arbitrary and meaningless in themselves. The magic of poetry creates these signs by purifying and cleansing (as in Sophia's bowl) words of their everyday meaning. As a consequence, the scribe's words about the piece of iron he had discovered, words describing it as a compass, were erased and only Fable's words about the effects of the uroboros made by Ginnistan were allowed to remain on the paper. Novalis sought through poetry to create word signs that had no fixed or definite referent, like those in the languages of algebra and music.

Once these words were freed from their customary or everyday referents, the poet could play with them, like a child with alphabet blocks, and make new combinations. Novalis wrote that poets and physical scientists have the same task—"to recast the world by developing new imaginative combinations." [26] For him, experimentations with poetic images in the imagination were analogous to experimentations in the physical sciences. The important point is that words in poetry, like mathematical signs in physical sciences, are not direct copies of reality; they do not mimetically represent things. Rather, they serve as arbitrary symbols with which the poet can delve beneath appearances and the given order of things and create a new order. The logical conclusion of this theory is that poets should write works like *Henry*. They should tell fairy tales and not merely reproduce reality as it is by copying it in a representational form of art.

Now we can see why Novalis thought poetry and dreams of the blue flower could be revolutionary. For the Enlightenment men who made discoveries in the physical sciences, the arbitrary, man-made mathematical signs were not the immediate representation of what they sought to understand but only the means by which they could chart the operation of an underlying universal order and law. They were confident of their efforts because they believed that a mind, a divine mind, had already reached into the chaos of life and formed his own rational order from it. Fichte had this confidence and more. For him man was not merely the discoverer of the universal order. This universal order was innate in his mind and he could know it in self-reflection and create images, prototypes, of it. Moreover, he could then reach into the chaos of human life and form his own order from it. But for his project to be successful, words, which were only necessary for communication, not for true knowledge, had to be tied to this true thought. Scholars had to control the use of these signs of communication and work to clarify their origin in man's intent, as Fichte himself had done with Pestalozzi's words.

The poetic system of arbitrary signs in *Henry* could never serve to order anything in a scholarly way, for no divine or philosophically self-reflective mind has reached into the chaos of life in this fairy tale and formed his own order from it. Mothers and the blue flower get in the way. In that life, all change and movement, all creating of society, comes through the mediation of fluids and woman's desire.

Novalis did agree with Fichte on one point. To discover the "truth," one had to turn inward. To do this, the poet, like Henry, had to learn to be independent of external stimuli and to replace external physical impressions with phychic ones. But in sharp contrast to Fichte's findings in self-reflection, Novalis found sensuous dreams, dreams of the blue flower in which the poet-dreamer is immersed in primordial fluids. Thus just as Fable spins truth from inside her body, the poet must reach inside. He must reach back, way back, into the source of life, to a fundamental psychobiological energy, to his feminine soul. In touch with this soul, he can then practice his magical "art of arbitrarily using the physical world." [27]

Is this just vitalist madness? Maybe so. But is it any more mad than Fichte's notion of reaching into his mind for the true ideas by which to rationally control the social world? Certainly not. Contemporary women-centered feminists are arguing that Fichte's madness worked. The male's pleasurable imagination of prototypes has had material effects in our world and on our bodies. As confused and crazy as the dreams of the blue flower may be, they at least free the imagination and engender the pleasure that seeks to transform society in cooperation with an infinitely creative material life force. This is a pleasure that seeks, not control over nature, but the potential to produce bodies that can be endlessly responsive to each other.

The difference between the views of Fichte and Novalis can be summed up by de Beauvoir's distinction between a clergyman or priest and a magician or poet. The priest "controls and directs forces he has mastered in accord with the gods and the laws [or if he is modern, with the laws and without the gods], for the common good, in the name of all members of the group; the magician operates apart from society, against the laws and the gods, according to his own deep interest." [28] Because women are not full members of the group, it is natural for them to be magicians, to oppose man's "bold emprise of transcendence" and to drag him into the shades of "immanence." [29]

In *Henry* those shades of immanence are lively ones filled with the transformative fluids and powers of women. But for Christian clergymen, "the destiny of man's soul is played out in regions where the mother's powers are abolished. . . . Maternity as a natural phenomenon confers no power." [30] If she wants to be deified by clergymen, de Beauvoir explained, women must subject themselves, by way of obedience to man, to God.[31]

Schleiermacher's Suppression of Sophia

The father of modern liberal Protestant theology, Friedrich Schleiermacher, gave his own interpretation of the goddess Sophia in what is essentially a nineteenth-century housefather book: *Christmas Eve: A Dialogue on the Incarnation.* Like Fichte in his discussion of Pestalozzi's work in *Addresses to the German People,* Schleiermacher appeared to clarify rather than deny Novalis's conception of the feminine soul; but again the result is suppression—suppression of a vision of feminine divinity and the new order based on that vision.

Christmas Eve was written in 1806, the year in which France occupied Berlin. The dialogue takes place in a salonlike atmosphere at a house party. But in contrast to the actual salons Schleiermacher had frequented in which feelings got out of hand and Jews, especially Jewish women, and Christians mingled together, in this imaginary salon everyone has a proper mate (except the single male skeptic guest, who is too busy doubting what he sees and hears to be bothered with passion) and everyone is Christian.

In Schleiermacher's story, Sophia becomes Sophie, a precocious child, who is the focus of the action and conversation at her parents' Christmas Eve party. The adults' observations and discussions of the child's actions evolve into salon talk, first about the childlike essence of women and then about the meaning of the Christ Child. Following the practice in the salons of that day, the men and women talk to each other, but in the story the discourse between the sexes is patterned according to their differences. The women tell Christmas stories and the men enter into a philosophical dialogue about the reality and meaning of the incarnation of Christ.

The result of this dialectic of the sexes is the restoration of agape and the father's rule in this household kingdom and the restoration of the story of Christ to its normative status. In short, at this party, the veil is put back on Isis.

Novalis has a central presence at the party. Sophie sings his poetry about the Virgin Mary to accompany the women's tales, which like Fable's are spun out of their breasts. But here the creative internal fluid generating poetry is maternal sentiment and it produces, not fairy tales, but representational art. The women tell stories of actual mothers and children that serve to tie down to its everyday meaning the image of Mary and the Christ Child. There is no danger in this salon that the Virgin Mary will change into Sophia, Demeter, Aphrodite, or Isis. The child Sophie is the linchpin holding this image to a clear and certain meaning. All of the acts of the little priestess of her parents' Christmas Eve cult are in the service of Christ.

THE NARRATIVE OF *CHRISTMAS EVE*

During the party the child Sophie arranges a representation of Mary and the Christ Child. Like Novalis, she is interpreted as having attempted to be a Correggio; unlike Novalis, she is successful. Working with "one of those little mechanical panoramas designed to represent the story of Christmas by means of tiny carved figures which move within an appropriate setting, she worked to add her own touches." [32] She took "pains to employ flame and water through the whole composition. . . . Streams actually flowed, and fires flickered." [33] They flowed and flickered through representations of the history of Christ's life and Christianity. From Christ's life she included his baptism, and Golgotha and the mount of ascension and then scenes of Pentecost, "the destruction of the temple, and Christians ranged in battle against the Saracens over the holy sepulcher." [34]

In the midst of these scenes, the representation of the birth of Christ itself was hard to find. It could finally be discerned by the light of a "beam streaming down from one hidden source upon the infant's head and casting a reflection on the bowed face of the mother. In contrast to the wild flames on the other side [apparently a reference to the representation of the burning of the reformer Hus and of Luther's burning of the pope's orders], this mild splendor seemed like a heavenly over an earthly light." [35] Sophie's one self-confessed disappointment with the arrangement of this scene was that she, in contrast to Novalis when he constructed Eros's religious vision, had failed to bring in a rainbow. No wonder, for here there is no blue flower.

After she has shown her work to the guests, Sophie cries to her mother, "Oh, Mother, you might just as well be the happy mother of the divine babe! And you are perhaps sorry that you are not? And is this, do you suppose, why mothers would rather have boys?" [36]

It takes Sophie's mother, Ernestine, a while to respond to this spontaneous question bursting from the child's "angel" heart about the significance of Christ's maleness for mothers. At first, the guests, overwhelmed by the child's display of what seems to be spontaneous piety, spend a "few silent moments in which they all knew that the heart of each person was turned in love toward all the rest and toward something higher still." [37] Agape fills Sophie's father's house.

Ernestine finally answers Sophie's question about mothers and boys through what seems to be a circuitous route. In fact, it takes a whole discussion of mother love, gender differences, and the true meaning of religion to answer the question. In the end we learn that mother love produces sons who are fit to join the army.

One of the couples at the party is engaged and the fiancé speculates that the older married couples may envy the emotions he and his prospective bride feel. Sophie's father, Eduard, says that this is not the case because married love *and* mother love are the same as their premarital "rapture." In *Henry* the rapture of heterosexual love, which is the same as mother love, is unquestionably erotic. In Eduard's house, as under the housefather's rule, they are all agape. In fact, the fiancé-lover himself confides that when he takes his beloved in his arms, it is as if she "had been given to him" along with Christ, his redeemer.[38]

While agreeing with her husband's description of the nature of mother love, Ernestine finally answers her daughter's question. She says, "In a way I feel that [Sophie] did not say too much when she thought that I might well be the mother of the blessed child. For I can in all humility honor the pure revelation of the divine in my daughter, as Mary did in her son, without in the least disturbing the proper relation of mother to child." [39]

In effect, Ernestine says that Sophie is like Christ, that in Sophie, a girl, there is a pure revelation of the divine, and that she, a mother, is like the Virgin Mary. She does not say it directly, but the reader is led to think that she means that she would not rather have a boy child. Although much more restrained than Novalis's identification of the revelation of the divine in Sophia, is this identification enough like it to be something quite

new in the father's house? No, because the old rules
for the proper relation of mother and child are still
recognized, and these are strict and constraining.

One of the guests is a young woman, Agnes, who is
pregnant. Agnes reveals the constraint of these rules by
claiming that all mother love is the same—unselfish—and
to be unselfish means that mothers know how to discipline children. Ernestine agrees and adds that fathers
can learn something from this mother love—how to discipline their sons for whose education they are responsible. Boys must be trained to be physically fit and ef-
ficient because progress "is always bound up with hard
exertion and denial." Thus fathers must know how to
check a boy's "growing feeling of autonomy" and mothers can teach them how.[40]

Sophie's father responds to his wife's comment. "Of
course we recognize that you are meant to care for the
first pure kernels of childhood and to help them develop
before any corruption enters in. You are made that way." [41]
The rest of what he says speaks for itself: "Women who
devote themselves to this holy service fittingly dwell
within the temple, vestals watching over the sacred fire.
But we [men] must venture forth into the world in
strict array, practicing discipline and preaching penance,
or as pilgrims cleaving fast to the cross and girding ourselves with swords in order to seek out some holy object or sanctuary and to recover it." [42] If Eduard had
met the medieval knights that Henry met, the father
would have joined the army.

At this point, the reader of Schleiermacher's story
does not fully understand the relation between Sophie's
Christlike soul, mother love, and joining the army. In
fact, in a replication of the scene from Henry's evening
with the knights, music like that he heard from Zulima
and the serenity it brings interrupt the scene. All this
is precipitated by Leonardt, the male skeptic, who interrupts this discourse on parental roles in education by
saying that he is worried about Sophie's piety, claiming

that it could make her unfit for marriage. A girl so pious might become a Catholic and a nun or a celibate Protestant sister.

Sophie's parents assure Leonardt that there is nothing to worry about. Her piety is spontaneous and they do nothing to encourage it. It is natural because it is not tied to any particular doctrine or external thing. Hers is a spontaneous religious joy, a feeling of harmony, like that evoked by music. Her piety clarifies the details of even the Christian story, revealing that true religion is the feeling of harmony, of interconnection, between people beneath all their differences, even the differences of sex.

What is extraordinary is that now the pregnant Agnes speaks again and ties this religious feeling to the proper relation between mother and child and to a mother's unselfishness. She says, "How much can what is strictly personal or particular . . . give to a soul stirred in the moods of piety, or take from it?" [43] Leonardt responds that Agnes's serenity "just seems too awful for words" and "denies the facts of life." [44] How can she repress the personal when she is pregnant?

Agnes explains that the "purely personal" does not enter into mother love at all! Newborn babies, in fact, often die, but that should not disturb the serenity of the pregnant woman because "a mother's love is what is eternal in [women]; it is the fundamental chord of [woman's] being." [45]

Leonardt cannot believe that Agnes is really indifferent to the prospect that her child might die or that she might not have the opportunity of personally influencing and forming her child's development. Agnes answers that she would not be indifferent to a child's death, but she could maintain her serenity because she would know that the child's inner life or soul was not destroyed by death. But then she tells us the truth about mother love: "What can we [mothers] form actually? . . . [Our] love is directed toward what we believe

to be lovely and divine in [the child] already, what every
mother looks for in every movement of her child, as soon
as its soul begins to find expression." [46] Thus, mothers
and mother love do not form anything. Mothers and
mother love only tend what is already there, an inner
flame, a divinity, a higher spirit. As Eduard said, they
keep the flame alive until fathers can take over the education of their sons.

Ernestine comments on Agnes's theory of mother
love with approval: "Every woman is another Mary.
Every mother has a child divine and eternal, and devoutly
looks out for the stirring of the higher spirit within it.
And into such a love no fate can bring ruinous affliction;
nor do the pernicious weeds of material vanity spring up
to choke it." [47]

Finally, it is Leonardt who draws out the implications of an unselfish, impersonal mother love that forms
nothing in the child. If what Agnes and Ernestine say
is true, then without a doubt, he exclaims, "You would
be the heroines of this age—you precious idealistic mis-
tresses of [dreams and visions] with your contempt for
the actual and the particular" and for the life or death
of your child.[48] If what these women say is true, he continues, then "one should have to regret that your congregation is not stronger and that you lack able-bodied
sons to bear arms and to do battle for you. You should be
the true ladies of Sparta!" [49]

This kind of mother love is what Germans need at
the moment, a moment when the French have invaded
their soil, says Leonardt. Watch out, he says, mothers will
be tested to prove they can love that way, for "great forces
of destiny are stomping around our neighborhood." [50]

The enraptured fiancé has the last word. He tells
Leonardt to be quiet, that war is not women's business.
But he also tells him that he need not worry; when war
comes, the women will be true to their word. Their sons
will join the army. They will suppress their personal
feelings and unselfishly sacrifice the physical life of their

sons for the higher spirit of the nation. Neither Sophie
nor her mother has the power of Sophia in *Henry* to restrict war to a chess game or to turn intimate physical
relations into the rule of the kingdom.

A REVISED MARRIAGE MANUAL

Schleiermacher's depiction of women in *Christmas Eve*
effectively thwarted the vision of Novalis in *Henry* and
illustrates the new definition of women that came to be
accepted as the norm by the early nineteenth century.
In the housefather books and into the eighteenth century, woman was defined in terms of her status as a wife
subject to her husband's will. After that, woman was defined in terms of inner qualities of soul or psyche that
fitted her for her role in the middle-class nuclear family.
Clearly the women at Schleiermacher's Christmas Eve
party are perfect middle-class housewives and like Sophie
are angels in the house.

Although Gertrude in *Leonard and Gertrude* has a
soul, there is not a great deal that is "feminine" about it
in the nineteenth-century sense of the word. The rules
written on Gertrude's soul reflect the status definition of
woman (and all others), a person serving the will of the
father. Above all, Gertrude is to be quiet and serve others.
What is new about her soul is that it is not weak like the
soul of Eve; it is the purest and strongest soul in Bonnal.
What is also new is that it is the soul of a poor woman,
not the soul of a housemother who rules the servants.
But for all its newness, it lacks the thickness and the
psychological depth of the women's souls in Schleiermacher's tale.

The wives and husbands at the Christmas Eve party
are clearly characterized by the gender definitions that
became prevalent in the nineteenth century.[51] The women
at Schleiermacher's party are more spontaneously sympathetic, moral, and religious than the hardhearted Leonardt and even the other less hardhearted men. Moreover, the women and the child Sophie help men see the

meaning of religion through their innocence and childlike natures. In this role women might appear to approach the role of Gertrude, whose soul saved the village
from chaos and misery. But Gertrude's accomplishment
was based on a different perception of religion as well
as of women. Let us reexamine the perception of religion
presented by Schleiermacher.

Trying to understand the implications for moral development of the differences between men and women,
Agnes asks, "Is it really true that our first objects of de-
light as children have to be dropped behind before we
can attain to higher things? . . . Does life begin, then, with
a sheer illusion, in which there is no truth at all, nothing
enduring?" Is it true that men must be reborn to attain the higher things of life? Do they have to lose their
first childhood and gain a second by passing through
"nothing"? [52]

Ernestine answers that it is true that men pass
through "nothing" in their moral development because
there is a time when they lead a "wild sort of life," a
life of striving, "an indecisive, ever-changing grasping
and letting go." Women do not do this because the
whole course of their lives is already "indicated" in
childhood play.[53] Even when women come to know the
higher meaning of life, to "understand God and the
world," they express this "in those same precious trifles"
they used as children.

Her husband, Eduard, agrees with her, but he adds
that although it develops in them in different ways, men
and women have the same "spiritual nature." Men are
more reflective than women and that leads them into
"passionate conflict with the world." [54] Does this mean,
we wonder, that men's superior qualities of reason somehow legitimate their wildness? Does their strong power
of self-reflection somehow allow men out of the nursery
to struggle to shape the world according to their purposes? Eduard makes clear that women who are less reflective do not go through this period and thus stay in

touch with their childhood. The "one" nature characterizing humanity is constituted by the complementarity of these different ways.

Again, it is Leonardt who sees the implications of this theory of moral development. Men have to be converted, reborn, to a spiritual life and women do not. Leonardt could just as well have said that men have the need to develop a second nature, the one they have created for themselves in struggling with the world, and women do not.

Schleiermacher is thus revealed as a typical theologian and theoretician of gender differences of his age: He saw Christ like women.[55] Christ, in contrast to other men, did not need to be reborn because from his birth he had an innocence of soul that kept him in immediate union with the divine. In Schleiermacher's theology, Christ is not the sacrificial son of a God who needs his death on the cross to gain his victory in the battle against cosmic forces of evil. Rather, Christ is the prototypical human who, unlike Adam, never breaks his ties with God. Thus women and little Sophies can represent Christ because they never break their ties with the innocence of childhood. Women are more at home than men in the sphere of religion because women realize the Christlike ideal of remaining in harmony with God throughout life, whereas men must strive to attain it. And in their striving they get to battle forces of evil with a "wildness." But men need not worry about losing their soul—as long as there are women around, at home. Men can stay in touch with religion as long as women stay at home in its sphere. In this view of religion, Schleiermacher and other nineteenth-century thinkers restricted the place of religion in their lives even as they ostensibly acknowledged a greater role for women in religion and in the home.

In tracing the change of the feminine soul from *Leonard and Gertrude* to *Christmas Eve*, through *How Gertrude Teaches Her Children* and the out-of-control images of the divine powers of woman in *Henry,* we can see that the transition from Gertrude in Bonnal to Ernestine at her house party did not occur without a struggle—a struggle to tightly control the religious qualities that were granted to woman's soul for the benefit of autonomous man. Part of this struggle was also to control which women could have the feminine soul. Woman can have her own "autonomous" soul, which no longer has the defects of her medieval soul, as long as she is the angel in the home reproducing other angels like Sophie and tending the flame of man's unruly religious nature. She can have the religious soul as long as she gives up the male desire to forge a second nature out of nothing.

7

The Domesticated Feminine Soul in Mother and Play Songs

The derivation of religious needs from the infant's
helplessness and the longing for the father
aroused by it seems to me incontrovertible, especially
since the feeling is not simply prolonged from
childhood days, but is permanently sustained by the fear
of the superior power of Fate. I cannot think of any
need in childhood as strong as the need for the
father's protection.[1]

FREUD, *Civilization and Its Discontents*

If men and their circumstances appear upside down
in all ideology as in a camera obscura, this phenomenon
is caused by their historical life-process, just as the
inversion of objects on the retina is caused by
their immediate physical life.[2]

MARX, *The German Ideology*

The mother-child relationship is the essential
human relationship.[3]

RICH, *Of Woman Born*

In Of Woman Born, Rich contends that "even safely caged in a single aspect of her being—the maternal—[woman] remains an object of mistrust, suspicion, misogyny in both overt and insidious forms." [4] In this chapter we will examine an overt form of this suspicion of what would seem to be a very safely caged feminine soul. The fate of a popular pedagogical manual, *Mother and Play Songs*, written in 1843 by the founder of the kindergarten system, Friedrich Froebel, provides yet another example of the struggle to contain the religious qualities of the feminine soul. [5] Influenced by Pestalozzi's writings, Froebel in contrast to Fichte had high hopes for mothers. He wrote *Mother and Play Songs* for use in the kindergartens he began to open in 1837 and in the training centers for kindergarten teachers (whom he insisted be young women) he established in the 1840s. Again like Pestalozzi, he designed his book for the use of mothers in the home.

There are three reasons for looking at Froebel's work. First, he was deeply influenced not only by Pestalozzi but also by Novalis. Because Froebel repeated the themes of both authors in a systematic theory of moral development in *Mother and Play Songs*, we can see in a brief work the cultural significance of those aspects of women's experience that contemporary women-centered feminists find missing in liberating theory. Froebel clearly stressed the cultural importance of the reproduction of life and the caring labor of the mother, which Marx overlooked, and offered an interpretation of the separation of the boy child from the mother that is quite different from Freud's Oedipal theory. Moreover, in an argument that anticipates Carol Gilligan's recent work, Froebel described the morality implied in women's experiences of childbirth and mothering—the reality of our interdependencies on one another, an awareness that "things unseen undergo change through time" and that "the boundaries between self and other" are not as sharp as the masculine ideals of autonomy and the control of nature define them.[6]

Second, Froebel was also deeply influenced by Schleiermacher and thus presented a feminine soul that is caged in the maternal far more securely than Novalis's feminine soul. Like the theologian, Froebel wrote of mothers tending the flames, or, as he puts it, germs of the divine in their babies. *Mother and Play Songs,* like *Christmas Eve,* seems to be a perfect expression of the gender ideology that prepared women for service in the home and trained them to be mothers of sons who joined the army. In a romantic prose worth quoting, Froebel wrote:

> Family Life! You are the sanctuary of humanity. You are the holy of holies for the nurture of the divine essence. Let it be said plainly and openly. You are more than school and church, and therefore more than all the institutions established for the protection of rights and property.... Family, without you, what are the altar and church if you do not consecrate them and elevate soul, heart, feeling and spirit, sentiment and thought, all of them yours, to the altar and temple of the one living God?[7]

It is the feminine soul in its maternal form that is the sanctuary within the sanctuary. At the end of this praise to the home sanctuary Froebel asked the key question: What is the military "unless you sanctify and justify" it? Thus *Mother and Play Songs* presents the dangers to women of believing in the feminine soul. It raises the questions that still must be asked even after recognizing other writers' suppressions of belief in the feminine soul. Like *Christmas Eve,* it raises the questions of whether the feminine soul is a class-bound ideal, a trap, a lure to the penumbra of men's violent history making, or a sign of something far greater.

The third reason for looking at *Mother and Play Songs* is that it was suppressed. In 1851 the Prussian government banned Froebel's kindergartens and his theory. Let us look first at Froebel's work and then at the efforts to suppress it.

The Content of Mother and Play Songs

Mother and Play Songs is both a theory of early childhood education and a theory of man's moral and religious development. Union with God is the ultimate purpose of all education and development. Froebel tells his female readers that when they arrive at "the goal of its education your child will know . . . the being and life and activity of God in all and through all." [8] The child will attain "a consciousness of the connectedness and unity of life," "a presentiment and feeling of God as the Eternal Fountain of Life." [9] This image of God as eternal fluid, although far more tame than Novalis's images, gives us a hint that Froebel's theory will not follow established belief.

In this theory, mothers are the mediators of the knowledge of God, and *Mother and Play Songs* is a guide for this mediation. The text is composed of a series of nursery rhymes. Each rhyme is complemented by a prescribed set of gentle physical exercises for the limbs of the baby or young child, a song, and a holy picture of a mother and child, which mothers or surrogate mothers in kindergartens are instructed to contemplate and to train their children to see. There is no doubt that Froebel, in contrast to Fichte, recognized the importance to moral and religious development of the time when the mother plays with her baby and talks baby talk. But it is also as though he can admit this only so long as he controls the mother's talk and touching.

Like the women Schleiermacher describes at the Christmas Eve party, Froebel thinks that the nature and purposes of God are revealed by the human phenomenon "with the deepest meaning," the phenomenon of mother and child. The divine, he contends, is revealed by the phenomenon of "motherhood and infancy in their inmost unity and reciprocity during the time when we are nursed at the breast." [10] Gazing on the phenomenon of mother and child, Froebel takes up what he thinks is a task neglected by most Christian theologians—making explicit the theological meaning of "these regions of experience." [11] By analyzing these experiences, Froebel discovers that God is "the inner unity of all being," [12] "the loving power that works everywhere in nature." [13]

Like Schleiermacher's theology, Froebel's system of salvation spun from his meditation on mother and child differs from that presented in orthodox Christian theology, which describes salvation through the relations of a father and son. In making explicit the truth that he considers implicit in the communing of the mother's soul with her child's and in the mother's instincts, Froebel claims that the human mother with her child is the savior of humanity. Salvation is granted through birth from the mother and sealed by her nurture of the child. God as creator is not an offended father who needs to be appeased through the obedient and sacrificial death of his son but rather the ever-fertile source of the "germs" of life, "germs" that can only be fully developed when nurtured by mother love. God immediately grants and grounds "the possibility of perfect humanity" and brings this humanity to fulfillment through the mother. And mothers in their souls have the intuition and vision of the "whole human essence, an essence destined for perfection" and possessed by their babies.[14]

CARING LABOR AND FALSE IDEAS

In Froebel's theory of moral development the only equivalent to evil is false knowledge, which takes the form of misperceptions and misinterpretations that mar human life.[15] Froebel calls this false knowledge "contradictions" between "heaven and earth" or, like Gilligan, contradictions between "things seen and unseen." Mother love is the antidote to this evil for it can correct these false ideas.

Like Fichte and the other German idealists, Froebel thought that true knowledge involved more than the impress of sense data or phenomena on the mind; rather it involved seeing beyond the outward forms of things into their universal truth. For the philosophers, this universal truth was ultimately an idea, the product of a mind, of an absolute spirit.

In his description of ideology, Marx likened this philosophical idealism to religion in its potential to hide from the oppressed the truth of their own powers and conditions. These philosophers, said Marx, legitimate the conditions that give them the power to dominate and oppress others by claiming that these conditions are incarnations of true ideas. Yet Marx, like these idealists, also thought that clear perception of true potentials and conditions entailed seeing beyond appearances into the essence of phenomena. Marx held that what was blocked at the level of appearances was the recognition of the human labor and the relations between men that produced things, the commodities of capitalist economy, and the social relations of the state.

Froebel expressed the same premise about perception by contending that if perception is blocked at the level of appearances, the interrelatedness of phenomena remains opaque. If it is blocked, things, people, and experiences falsely appear as discrete entities and events. Separation and distinction are mistaken for the truth. What Froebel thought was blocked at the level of appearances was the recognition of the caring labor that binds people and phenomenon together. Mother nurture alone ensures that man does not mistake for the truth the disunity he experiences within himself, the separations he experiences between himself and others, and the conflicts he experiences between himself and physical nature. Only a vision trained by the nurture of the

mother can see beyond appearances of separation to the
truth of men's interdependence, to the truth of the in-
terconnectedness of all things, and ultimately to love as
the foundation of connectedness.

In contrast to Marx, who thought religion cooperated with the philosopher's effort to mask the actual labor
and interdependence of people, Froebel concluded that
the criticism of religion created the mask. Only a religion
engendered at the mother's breast can bring clear perception. In an intimate unity with the mother, the child has
an intuition of the truth of interrelation, an intuition
that is the most religious of dreams. It is the critique of
this childhood dream as illusion that causes human error
and leads to ineffective action.[16] Froebel, unlike the men
in Schleiermacher's *Christmas Eve,* did not think that
men have to lose this dream. It is only because it is falsely
treated as an illusion and "torn" from men that men's
mature years are marked by lack and emptiness, by nothing. When it is torn from them, men lose the knowledge
of the truth engendered by mother love altogether, or
regaining it "too late, they have already lost the most
beautiful and richest part of life and its most pleasurable
experiences." [17]

There is no question that Marx would have rejected
the mystical and dreamy musings of Froebel. Yet he
might have valued the sort of vision engendered by
mother love. Froebel describes the effects of mother love
on the perception of the male child when, as was proper,
his father introduced him to the world of commerce.
When the boy child, who is trained as a seer by his
mother, is taken by his father to the marketplace, he
immediately recognizes the commodities as human-made
products, not merely as things to be possessed or traded.
The boy child sees in them "the needs and essence" of human. What his mother's nurture has done is provide him
with an inner mirror that reflects not merely the surface
of things but what is behind them. "Gazing into this
mirror," when looking at commodities, the boy child sees

in them "his own physical and spiritual potential." [18]
This mirror given by the mother is different from the
obscuring ideological mirror that Marx described as reflecting the true dynamic of society upside down.[19]

In comparison with the various liberating theories, Froebel's theory differs most sharply from Freud's theory of
child development. Like Pestalozzi, Froebel described a
separation from the mother that is necessary but does not
sever the bonds of unity between the mother and child.
The mother of the infant and of the man can remain
all in all without crippling the individual's development.
It is true, Froebel wrote, that "the natural and original
bond, the existence of the unity of the child with the
mother's heart, love, and activity, can be misunderstood"
and that a mother must put "wholesome limits" on it.
But he immediately added, "If this unity, when misunderstood, brings injury, how much more is brought by
separation when it is confused, misinterpreted, and misunderstood." [20] Just imagine how much more injury is
brought when men like Fichte, Freud, and the housefathers make that separation the premise of moral development.

According to Froebel, the mother initiates games of
hide-and-seek to introduce wholesome limits on her physical intimacy with the child, but at the same time she
takes care to avoid the danger that he might learn to
enjoy keeping himself and his deeds hidden from the
mother.[21] Played correctly, the games teach the child
through periods of physical separation and return how
to heighten his sense of spiritual union with his mother.
The length of time the child can remain hidden corresponds with his "rising tide of consciousness." [22] But here
the growing sense of consciousness, which is a consciousness of a separate self, does not result in a loss of the
mother and her nurture. It results in an intensified de-
light in finding the mother and in the realization that

physical separation cannot sever the bonds of her love. For the boy child the necessary and important development of the full powers of his mind and self-consciousness corresponds with a heightened realization of the definitive meaning of his early physical union with his mother. Proper child development leads to a respect for and pleasure in life.

For Froebel, then, the phenomenon of mother and child is the prototype, a ground in which all other phenomena of life find their essence or truth. It is a prototype men can see in reality, not one they must imagine by turning inward in self-reflection. Yet in a sense man must go inward to find its full truth. In this case he must go into the soul of the mother. It is the loving soul in communion with the soul of her child that always serves as the undistorted mirror of reality and reflects the relations between what seem, in imperfect mirrors, to be isolated, disconnected entities. The phenomenon of mother and child directly reveals what is beneath the veil of appearances. Gazing on this phenomenon in maturity and recalling the dreams of unity it engenders in infancy, man perceives the reality of relation beneath apparent truth of the isolations and conflicts of life.

GOD AS MOTHER

In contrast to Pestalozzi, Froebel never called God a mother. He tended to use abstract terms or metaphors, like the eternal fountain of life, for God, and he did not hesitate to call God father. Nonetheless it does not take much imagination to find a female God in *Mother and Play Songs*. The pictures accompanying each nursery rhyme are holy pictures of mothers who have the stature of goddesses. There is no doubt that in telling mothers and surrogate mothers what to see in these pictures Froebel sought to control the child's vision of the mother, just as he tried to control the mother's talk to and touch of her child by giving her rhymes and exercises.

Almost all of the pictures are shaped like a medieval

altar, with the mother and child in the place of the holy of holies, in the center of the sanctuary. For example, the familiar game pat-a-cake is illustrated with an image of a mother with a child on her lap, seated in the center of a busy kitchen that is framed by two towering inserts on the upper left-hand and right-hand sides. In one insert is the image of a woman rolling dough and in the other are three children playing with mud cakes outside in a lush green setting with a church steeple in the background. Cuckoo, Cuckoo, a rhyme in baby talk, is illustrated by a mother sitting outside in an arbor with the setting sun appearing through the arch as a halo. Her child is peeking out from under her cape and the mother's head is lovingly bent down toward him. Two other children play on either side of her. In what is perhaps the most striking image, which follows Froebel's long introductory remarks on childbirth, the mother assumes the pose of the Virgin Mary most often chosen for Pietás. But here the mother looks serenely at her sleeping baby, not sorrowfully at her dead son. All of the mothers imaged in *Mother and Play Songs* are full-figured, robust, and smiling. Most are depicted outside the home in the midst of lush natural, nearly cosmic settings. The few who are indoors inhabit open spaces, in front of wide windows, for example, through which vast expanses of nature are visible and vibrant light shines. Dressed in loose, flowing gowns, they resemble the triumphant Italian Renaissance madonnas of Raphael and Correggio far more than egg-faced, ringleted bonneted fragile girls produced by a domesticated romanticism. Outside in their cosmic spaces, with a little imagination they even seem to resemble Isis.

Rich invites us to look at images of goddesses that men created and to try to imagine what they conveyed to women.[23] She says, "If they did nothing else for her, they must have validated her spirituality (as our contemporary images do not), giving her back aspects of herself neither insipid nor trivial, investing her with a sense of the participation in essential mysteries." [24] Rich goes on to say that no Pietà could do this. Yet Froebel's Pietàs did. In the company of the other images, Froebel's substitution of the live baby for the dead son could easily have given women ideas. Surely we can conclude that if these images did nothing else for women, they would have made it hard for them to imagine God as a father.

The Suppression of Mother and Play Songs

In 1851 the Prussian minister of education issued an edict banning the kindergartens and Froebel's theories as subversive to the state. It is important to keep in mind that this was a state still reacting to the revolution of 1848, and thus a state hostile to any democratic or socialist theories or movements. In the 1810s Prussia and the other German states had been successful in driving the French troops from their soil, and they had been successful because they had persuaded ordinary men to join professional soldiers in the army. During the next three decades, dramatic economic and social changes occurred as a result of increased industrialization, but the German states did not undergo corresponding political change. Prussia and the other states, although entertaining the establishment of constitutional and representative governments, retained the rule of monarchs and aristocrats, and in 1848 a widespread, but ultimately unsuccessful, revolution took place. In 1851 the political mood was reactionary.

The Prussian minister's edict conflated Friedrich Froebel's work with that of his nephew Karl Froebel, who openly espoused socialist theories. While his uncle mused on the souls of mothers and opened kindergartens, Karl was busy promoting higher education for women as a necessity in an egalitarian society. The edict declared that both high schools for women and kindergartens for children were centers for training in atheistic socialism.[25]

Horrified at being called an atheist, Friedrich Froebel
protested what he saw as a confusion of his theories with
his nephew's, and sent his writings to the minister of education. After reviewing them, the official held his ground.
He said that Froebel's kindergarten theory placed "at the
foundation of the education of children a highly confused and disordered and complex theory" that was as
alien to Christianity as Karl Froebel's clearly atheistic
socialism.[26] Notice how the minister, like Fichte, used the
term *confusing* for a theory of the preeminence of the
spiritual qualities of the mother. To confuse people about
religious truth was as heretical as an open denial of God.
The religious truth Froebel's theories confused was that
of the centrality of the relationship of father and son.

Baroness Bertha von Marenholtz-Bülow, Froebel's
devotee, explained that Prussia suppressed the kindergartens because Froebel's method departed from "the
morbid [Christian Lutheran] Pietism" espoused by its
officials.[27] There is no doubt that Froebel's theory of
moral development and the theology implicit in it would
have been blatantly heretical from the point of view of
the Christian Pietists politically influential in his day.
In reaction to the positive view of human nature articulated in theologies like Schleiermacher's, which they saw
as promoting the struggle for human rights, the Pietists
stressed the doctrine of original sin, especially the belief
that it created a rift between man and God that man is
unable to overcome alone. Only through the obedient
death of God's son on the cross is salvation and reunion
with God the father possible. In this system of salvation,
then, Christ through his death is the mediator between
the sinful human and God. Like the authors of the housefather books, the Pietists held that only Christ's male
representatives on earth, in the church and state and in
the family, are mediators of the divine will. Here there
is not even a place for Schleiermacher's caged feminine
soul.

The Baroness also explained that these religiously

conservative government leaders considered any sort of grass-roots education of the people "the most dangerous weapon in the hands of revolution." [28] Education by mothers is the most basic of all education and these leaders did not believe in its benefits for the state any more than did Fichte. Finally, the Baroness recorded Froebel's radical assertion that, despite his own intense religious piety, allied him with his nephew Karl: "Those considered minors and dependents in our time should come of age, and these are above all women and children, whose human dignity has not been recognized until now for its full worth." [29] Thus, despite Froebel's claim that mother love in the family sanctified and legitimated the military and all the institutions of the state, Prussian officials did not believe him.

To illustrate how strongly the tide flowed against Froebel's theory, let us look briefly at a theory of education that became popular in Germany in the 1850s. This was the theory of Daniel Schreber, the father of Judge Schreber whose memoirs Freud analyzed in generating his theories of paranoia. Daniel Schreber was an advocate of gymnastic training of the body. He was noted for designing harnesses and other restraining devices to force children to develop proper posture. This advocate of physical discipline wrote, "[It is] especially important and crucial for the whole of life with regard to character . . . to form a protective wall against the unhealthy predominance of the emotional side, against that [effeminate sentimentality]—the disease of our age, which must be recognized as the usual reason for the increasing frequency of depression, mental illness, and suicide." [30] Schreber's antidote for a femininity that had gotten out of hand was the promotion of the truth that the "basic condition of life is a fight," a battle between reason and "innate barbarity." [31] When the child is six months old, the father should begin to suppress all effeminate sentimentality in the child. To do this, the father should lead the child in physical drills and force him to take physical risks. Schreber sum-

marized his wisdom for early childhood education: "Better to have a temporarily injured hide or a bruise than
an eternally injured and weak soul." [32] In a society that
preferred this form of training for children there could
be little room for a theory based on maternal love.

The text of *Mother and Play Songs,* belief in the
maternal soul, and even the kindergarten system survived
the Prussian suppression, but Froebel's theology did not.
Froebel died in 1852, but the Baroness continued to promote the kindergarten movement and she succeeded in
her vigorous fight to have the ban lifted in 1860. Moreover, Froebel's kindergarten theory spread to the United
States, where he had hoped to take it after its suppression
in Prussia. Unfortunately, Froebel's theory encountered
the same hostility and suspicion in the United States. An
American pedagogue wrote in 1916: "[Froebel's] mother-
play book as a whole is not a safe book to put in the
hands of mothers or of kindergarten novitiates." [33] Like
Fichte responding to Pestalozzi, pedagogues could see the
value in some of the practices of Froebel's early childhood
education, for example, in the physical exercises for babies, but they found his complete theory of child development confusing and dangerous. To place transformative
cultural potential in the feminine maternal soul was revolutionary. Both the Prussian minister of education and
the American pedagogue had to reject *Mother and Play
Songs.*

It was safe and socially beneficial to develop what one
Froebel follower in 1869 called a *science* of the maternal
soul, that is, a female psychology that posited a maternal
instinct in the psyches of women. In other words, it is
safe to have a science that defines women in terms of
maternity. But it is not safe to have what might be called
a theology of the maternal soul, a theory that ties moral
qualities to a divine referent, a divinity that in turn could
be imagined as a female God.

To understand what happens to the belief in the
feminine soul when it is no longer permitted to reach to

a female God, let us imagine Froebel's holy pictures without the transcendent reality of nurture. What would happen if in place of the mystical, loving fluid God we placed the reality defined by Schreber, the reality of a battle between barbarity and reason? The cosmic spaces inhabited by the holy women would close up and the mother goddesses would retreat behind walls to become powerless angels while outside raged the fight that is now the true condition of life.

8

Religion, Gender, and Ideology: A New Theory

*There is no reason to exclude the possibility of radical
transformations of behavior, mentalities, roles, and
political economy. . . . Let us imagine simultaneously
a* general *change in all the structures of formation,
education, framework, hence of reproduction, of
ideological effects, and let us imagine a real
liberation of sexuality, that is, a transformation of
our relationship to our body (—and to another body),
an approximation of the immense material organic
sensual universe that we are, this not being
possible, of course, without equally radical political
transformations (imagine!).*[1]

HÉLÈNE CIXOUS, *"The Newly Born Woman"*

In DESCRIBING THE POSSIBILITY of radical cultural transformations, Cixous invites us to imagine. Like the other women-centered feminists, she invites us to imagine the powers of women outside the old order, which is the present order of dominations of the logic of identity, the death culture in which human life is held hostage to the superpowers' will and their logic of nuclear deterrents.[2] Like Rich and Daly, Cixous invites woman who is "still foundering" in the old order to imagine her power and to express the genius or soul of her own body.

The invitation to imagine the power of woman is the root of the new theory of religion, gender, and ideology that these women-centered feminists are offering us. Here its meaning will be drawn out in relation to the local German history of belief in the feminine soul we have traced. First, we will return to Hester Eisenstein's accusation that these feminists are offering us a spirituality instead of a politics. Then we will examine the perception of the material power of ideology held by these feminists. Finally, we will look at their new theory of religion, gender, and ideology and how it differs from the theory of religion and politics that men claim has produced a religious crisis in the West.

The Separation of Spirituality and Politics

Eisenstein contends that in stressing women's unique experience and potential the extreme women-centered feminists are turning their backs on our Western liberating traditions of liberalism, Marxism, and psychoanalysis. Thus instead of offering us a radical politics, the feminists are offering us a reactionary one. By inviting women to imagine, to dream their own dreams, to have their own visions, women-centered feminists seem to be luring women away from a political realism and a concrete struggle with male-dominated structures into a separate inner space of spirituality. In discussing Mary Daly's

Gyn/Ecology, for example, Eisenstein says that Daly carries "women-centered analysis to its logical conclusion." In affirming women's difference, Daly names "rationality, linearity, logic and science" as male and refuses the validity of the reformation of a culture already based on male thought and systems. "Urging women instead to embark on an inner journey of discovery" and to embrace "female difference," Daly seems to call them to a "withdrawal from political struggle," to an apolitical separatist spirituality.[3]

Eisenstein admits that political realism must be joined with a certain degree of utopianism, a certain degree of dreaming the possible. But this utopianism should not go so far as to take the form of a new religion, which for Eisenstein means a belief in a metaphysical female essence. This belief is, in fact, an old belief, an old male illusion. In Eisenstein's view, women's utopianism should take the form of an attempt to transform Western liberation theory by imbuing it with "the woman-centered values of nurturance and intimacy, as necessary and legitimate goals of political life." [4]

After tracing the history of belief in the feminine soul, we can see that spirituality and politics are not as easily separated as Eisenstein's analysis suggests. We have seen that men's embarking on inner voyages of discovery, their embrace of male difference, and their separatism in the public sphere has had concrete social, political, and economic effects. Women-centered feminists' dreams of the power of women are not apolitical dreams. If nothing else, they are dreams that recover the political meanings of male dreams about the transformative cultural potential of intimacy and nurture. At times these meanings were carried by a male's belief in a version of the feminine soul, but they were suppressed in the production of our Western liberation theories. Some of the men who tried to describe the moral development of politically mature man recognized the social, political, and even cosmic significance of nurture and intimacy, and they located the powers of nurture and intimacy in the female body and the feminine soul—and, at times, in a female God. Other men suppressed the significance of nurture and intimacy either by severely limiting them to the small circle of the home and nursery, as did Schleiermacher, or by denying them altogether in favor of the autonomous ego of man by which he could determine his historical fate and control nature, as did Fichte. Behind all these suppressions lurked the old Christian story of the weakness of woman's soul and the necessity of the rule of the father.

In essence, theoreticians of man's liberation like Rousseau, Fichte, Kant, and Schleiermacher divorced spirituality, a spirituality that was different from that of the religion of God the father and his sons, from politics. Yet even as they criticized the religion of God the father, they kept elements of its spirituality for their politics. They wanted cultural maturity and freedom from God the father, the sin of Adam, and the need for imitating the sacrificial obedience of Christ. They demanded the right to determine their own political fate free from the rule of God the father's divinely ordained representatives on earth. They claimed the right to create their own nature free from the need to receive a second nature through God the father's grace and forgiveness won for them by Christ's death. They claimed the right to define the operations of their spiritual and physical nature free from the myths of God's supernatural powers by which he intervened in their world.

Nonetheless, not unlike those men who clung to the truth of the traditional Christian story in the hope of retaining old political privileges, such as the government leaders in mid-nineteenth-century Prussia, they were not willing to give up the powers of this God. They wanted them for themselves. Perhaps, more than anything, they wanted to exercise his powers of dominance over nature by virtue of their absolutely free will, and they wanted to take over his role in the battle against the forces of evil and barbarity. Even a theologian like Schleiermacher, who feminized Christ and abandoned the story of God's cosmic battle against evil, reserved the right of earthly battle and the privilege of creating a second nature for men.

The originators of modern liberating theory who went so far as to identify God the father as an illusion were no different. They too told the old story. Freud told it brashly. He located man's moral development in the Oedipal phase and defined moral maturity in terms of identification with and internalization of the father. This internalization of the human father replicated, according to Freud, primordial man's internalization of the illusory divine father, who represented the real father they murdered in order to possess his sexual privilege with the mother. Freud reasoned that because a female's Oedipal development was different from a male's, because ultimately she internalized her mother, not her father, her conscience or superego was weaker than the male's. Women are thus inevitably drags on civilization.

Marx's retention of the old story is manifest most clearly in his complicity with the Christian clergy in seeing the destiny of man played out in regions where "maternity as a natural phenomenon confers no powers." [5] His own critique of religion was formulated in terms of Luther's transfer of religious autonomy to housefathers, not in terms of Pestalozzi's transfer of religious autonomy to poor women. There is no doubt that Marx had no sympathy for the religion of the mother-lover that Novalis created to expose the nature of the religion of the Philistines and that heretically called into question the truth of the Christian system of salvation through the relations of the father and son. Marx did not see that Novalis's religion could alienate people from given conditions and thereby create the possibility for their transformation, rather than serving, as did the religion of God the father, to ensure social and political stasis. In fact, Marx railed against what he saw as the "effeminate resignation" of such a cult and saw its meaning limited to "the Sunday walks of an inhabitant of a small provincial town who childishly wonders at the cuckoo laying its eggs in another bird's nest." [6] We can imagine that for Marx, Froebel's image of the divine mother babbling "cuckoo, cuckoo" with her baby would have signified small circles of unproductive life and a primitive childlike regressive naturalism very like the primitive regressive mother love the housefathers relegated to housemothers. The mother could not represent culture for Marx.

All our modern liberation theories, in one way or another, linked man's quest for justice and freedom to his recognition that the dominant Western religion of God the father and his sons was, either in part or in whole, illusory and exploitative—that some, if not all, of man's religious beliefs were products of his imagination that mistakenly attributed to God man's own powers for determining his existence and shaping his world. In the process, they also rejected the heretical religion of a female God because, it too, misidentified their powers. In fact, in contrast to the religion of God the father, the religion of a female God was not even a product of man's ordinary imagination. It did not reflect his powers, even in the upside-down ideological fashion Marx described. Thus these liberating theoreticians dismissed it as the product of a mad or confused male imagination—and sexuality.

If women looked back into history and found only the religion of the father and son, then we might say that Eisenstein is correct in urging feminists to abandon spirituality in favor of politics. But history contains threads of another religion, that of the mother and the feminine soul.

The Power of the Definition of the Feminine Soul

At times the complex imaginations of Novalis and Pestalozzi came close to producing a theory of the woman's body and its relation to language identical to the theory later developed by contemporary women-centered feminists. These men came close to describing the subversion of the logic and definitive lawful words of the father by the different language that emerges from the reality of the female body. They came close to describing an "ultimate reality" marked by the continual fluidity of finite forms, the experience of a unity that generates, rather than represses, difference, and the primordial truth of nurture. But only close.

While it is true that contemporary feminists are recovering what can be called a subjugated historical knowledge of the transformative potential of the feminine soul, they are doing more than recovering a rare male imagination. Contemporary women-centered feminist theory cannot be reduced to the recovery or repetition of a historically suppressed male theory, because now women themselves are assuming control of the belief in the feminine soul. Now *they* are doing the imagining and, in doing so, are offering us a new interpretation of religion, gender, and ideology that has radical political meanings.

Historians like Rowbotham and Hausen have used the tools of the critique of religion as ideology that pervades Western liberating theory to identify ideals of the feminine soul as products of male imagination that served as instruments of social control of women in male-dominated Western society. Contemporary women-centered feminists are fully aware of the illusory nature of the heritage of ideas about woman's unique feminine soul. They do not believe, as did those eighteenth- and nineteenth-century men who lauded the feminine soul, that there really *is* an eternal, transhistorical feminine essence or soul in any traditional metaphysical or religious sense. Yet they believe that the feminine soul is real, that it is more than a male illusion.

Women know the reality of this soul from experience, their experience of its material power, under men's control, to shape their behavior and to determine their use of their bodies. On the basis of the all too real experience of the oppressive power of belief in a male-defined feminine soul, women-centered feminists claim that under their control this belief can have the material power to disrupt and to reshape Western culture.

In describing the pervasiveness in the West of the association of women's spirituality and motherhood, Rich says that when we think of motherhood, we are supposed to think of icons of Mary.[7] We are not supposed to think of how men tied these images to biopolitics and to infanticide.[8] We are not supposed to identify, as we have done, representations of the feminine soul as the creations of historical men for the service of their biopolitics. We are not supposed to understand how these men used ideological power to prevent infanticide and to force good mothering.

Women know from experience that this use of ideological power was successful; it had material effects. Many, many Western women have thought what they were supposed to think. To think of motherhood and the goodness of soul together has become habitual, so habitual that women have "accepted the stresses of the institution [of motherhood] as if they were a law of nature."[9] They do not recognize that the institution and the spirituality of motherhood are a second nature created for them by men in the service of their biopolitics.

As Rich puts it, women "do not think of the laws that determine how" women got to the "thousands of kitchens, in each of which children are being fed and sent off to school."[10] Women do not think of "the penalties imposed on those of us who have tried to live our lives according to a different plan, the art which depicts us in an unnatural serenity or resignation, the medical establishment which has robbed so many women of the act of giving birth."[11] To fully understand ideals of motherhood as ideology, we must examine the many channels of cultural authority by which they are carried and transformed into norms.

Among these channels, according to Rich, are the liberating theories, even those theories that criticize belief in metaphysical souls or essences. She says, "We do not think of the Marxist intellectuals arguing as to whether we produce 'surplus value' in a day of washing clothes, cooking food, and caring for children, or the psychoanalysts who are certain that the work of motherhood suits us by nature." [12]

To understand the belief in the male-defined feminine soul as ideological, then, we must identify all those secular and even purportedly scientific channels of influence and authority through which it has had concrete and material effects on women's bodies and behavior. We need to stretch the metaphor of the feminine soul all the way from that illusory metaphysical essence of women believed in by nineteenth-century romantic philosophers to the most scientific male psychologies of women in order to see the pervasiveness of its effects. To say that the feminine soul is a historical male illusion is clearly not enough.

Rich does not focus on the illusory nature of the ideals of motherhood or women's spirituality. Instead she focuses on how, under men's control, these ideals have robbed women of power by the way they have been institutionalized through the laws, arts, and social and psychological sciences. She focuses on "the power stolen from us and the power withheld from us, in the name of the institution of motherhood." [13]

The strategy she and other women-centered feminists adopt for the recovery of this power is to gain control "over the production, distribution and transformation of meaning," the meaning of the feminine soul. To these feminists this struggle is at least as crucial as the struggle "over economic and political power," that is, at least as crucial as resistance to the many structures that restrict women's power to men's biopolitics.[14] In a sense, these women have opted to treat the spirituality of the feminine soul as if it referred to something real by entering into

a struggle with male metaphysical and scientific definitions of that soul in order to define the reality to which
that soul refers. In the process, they are refusing to say
that the feminine soul as a spiritual ideal must serve as
an instrument for the social control of women. They
are wagering that under their control the feminine soul
can be a new and different religious ideal bearing the
promise of resistance to social control and of radical cultural transformation.

In the local German history of the feminine soul
we have examined, we have seen that even men's representations of its unique spiritual qualities were not as
safe as they might have seemed. The representation of
the feminine soul led some men to imagine that the
power of women as mothers and as lovers had political
and even cosmic meaning. It led some men to imagine
what life could be like if God were imaged as a female
and not as a judging father. But it led other men, even
those men who rejected God the father as an illusion,
to repeat the old story of woman's defective soul and
to ignore the material significance of reproduction and
caring labor.

By contrast, Rich and other women-centered feminists are asking, What will happen if women who struggle
free from the constraints of the institutionalization of
motherhood and femininity begin to imagine the power
of women as mothers and lovers? What would happen if
they took control of the representation of the feminine
soul? What would happen if the representation of the
feminine soul got out of hand, if it were wrenched free
from systems of male thought and even from those male
thinkers who, in a sense, conceived it?

Recognizing and struggling free from biopolitics today, women have "a possibility of converting our physi-
cality into both knowledge and power." [15] Women know
that man's knowledge is inextricably linked with this
power; his knowledge is shot through all those structures
in male-dominated society that oppress women. Thus

the empowerment of women cannot come merely from a struggle for social, political, and economic change. Women's power is also inextricably linked with her creation of knowledge, her own imagining.[16] Because of their recognition of the material power of ideas of the feminine soul over women's bodies rather than their belief in a metaphysical essence, radical women-centered feminists like Rich and Daly and the French feminists seem to be embracing a form of religion and along with it the feminine soul. They believe that if controlled by women speaking out of their liberated bodies, the feminine soul can become a representation that will disrupt male logic and the old order of death.

A New Theory

Mary Daly recognized long ago that mere rejection of God the father as an illusion was not enough to free women from social and political domination. Women had to go beyond God the father to find their own divine referent. If, on the one hand, women cannot accept the religion of God the father, on the other, they cannot accept man's reduction of religion to a material or psychological determinism or a "liberal" version of religion in which man's full autonomy coexists with a less authoritarian but still male God. Women cannot afford to cede religion either to man's control or to his criticisms. The death of God that the self-determining man of the modern West proclaimed cannot mean the death of religion for women.

The fundamental reason for this is that the humanity men found when they altered or rejected the reality of God the father was itself made in that God's image. Humanity, even that illusion-free self-determining humanity of modernity is male, as de Beauvoir said, because "man defines woman not in herself but as relative to him: she is not regarded as an autonomous being." [17] Humanity is male because woman "is defined and differentiated with reference to man and not he with reference to her; she is the incidental, the inessential. He is the Subject, he is the Absolute—she is the Other." [18] The definition of woman as man's inessential other is a crucial element in the Western male's criticism of religion as ideology. Just as the housefather theologians insisted that the religious human father is like God the father, so the most severe critics of the religion of God the father as ideology said that secular man is like God the father. Freud plainly says so in his description of the primordial murder of the father who became God and in his Oedipal theory. Let us examine now how the Marxist theory of religion as projection says so too.[19]

According to this theory, God is man's projection of his own *essential* qualities, that is, of his enormous and, indeed, infinite potential as a species that thinks, wills, and shapes its own nature by shaping physical nature for its own purposes. It is as if men made their gods by standing in front of a flattering mirror, a divinizing mirror that reflects only their difference from all other creatures, their difference from animals and—as we recognize but Marx did not—their difference from women. The mirror reflects the qualities that men think distinguish them as human, their thought and their will and their capacity to create a world from the "nothing" of matter by their fiats. Contemporary feminists point out that what men have seen in the divinizing mirror is both their biological difference from women and their spiritual or mental differences from animals—or their higher spiritual qualities of thought and will superimposed on their biological uniqueness—so that their distinct sexual characteristic is spiritualized and turned into a symbol of will and thought. The phallus becomes a symbol of power, and thus in man's divinizing mirror, his essential humanity and the God he images are phallocentric.

In man's individual and historical childhood, that is, in the time before he becomes self-conscious, he does not know that he is looking in a mirror. On the one hand, he believes that what he sees is really other than himself. But on the other, he naively and spontaneously identifies with the figure in the mirror. Having the sense that he is like the image, he shares in its powers. At this point, man's imaginary God is beneficial for him.

Religion and the making of gods, even phallocentric religion and male gods, become oppressive to men when they lose the sense of identification with their image and begin to see themselves as different from the God in the mirror. Then they define themselves in terms of what is not in the image, in terms of what they lack. Religion becomes oppressive when men see themselves as defined by what is not essentially and distinctively human, that is, by what they have in common with the animals— and women.

Religion becomes a tool of men's political and social as well as psychic oppression when some men retain the privilege of likeness to the God in the mirror and deny it to others. For men to submit to the rule of these select representatives of God, they must be forced to continue looking into the mirror. Their likeness to this imaginary God must not be totally denied; if it is, they will look away. To continue to respect the powers of the imaginary God and those men who are in his image, men must believe that though they are lacking these powers now, they will someday possess these powers.

There are many mechanisms by which men can be convinced of their own lack yet be enticed to worship the imaginary God and his earthly surrogates. Belief in heaven, in the possession of the powers after death, is the preeminent one. It persuades man to accept his powerlessness and limits here on earth in return for the promise of happiness in the hereafter. In all its oppressive forms, religion turns God and his representatives into absolute subjects and other men into their objects.

Inequality and domination flow from the belief in this God because his image is made by man's omission of what he associates with finitude, his animal body and its functions, especially biological reproduction. Although his own male reproductive organ distinguishing him from woman is imaged, it is spiritualized and associated with creation by the will. Everything in the image is based on differentiation. What was there "in the beginning" is not the one powerful phallic will and thought but something more—the rest of man, his finite body and the different body of woman. The very making of the God involves a differentiation that is hierarchical. Man's essential qualities are raised in front of the mirror and worshiped as his divine other and his inessential qualities are lowered beneath the mirror and despised as his finite other. The imaging of God as the one powerful phallic will and thought necessarily involves the identification of an other that is not the one.[20]

According to de Beauvoir, woman has filled the space of this other that is not the one, the space of man's inessential other. When a few men claim as their privilege identification with this one God, other men also fill this space. For the dynamic of this phallocentric religion demands a rejected object, a scapegoat, a group to fill the space of the inessential. To have the one will and thought of God as the norm of essential humanity, there must always be an inessential other.

Those few men representing God exercise his powers and do in fact create the world from their will and thought by defining its laws and the norm of humanity. All others must conform to the norm and, of course, obey the laws of this divinely ordained world—or be legitimate victims of its justice. As contemporary women-centered feminists point out, this justice can readily seem to be egalitarian. This justice can be expressed by the principle that all men are the same. But the sameness by which men are defined, their common possession of free will and thought, is also the norm by which others are oppressed. Defining this sameness always necessitates a differentiation that makes that sameness superior to what is not the same. Women, along with other human groups, have been relegated to what is not the same. They have been victimized or told to wait and behave until someday they can be the same.

Marx described men's liberation from the oppression of religion in terms of his waking up and realizing that God is nothing but his own image in the mirror. When he wakes up, he claims his essential human qualities as his own; he claims for himself the right and position of the subject.

Marx identified the oppression of men by religion in much the same way that de Beauvoir identified the oppression of women by men. Like women defined by men, men drugged by the opiate of religion are objects and victims of the absolute subject God and his representatives. Oppressed by religion, men like women are doomed by God and his representatives to the realm of immanence, to what de Beauvoir described as "stagnation . . . the brutish life of subjection to given conditions." This is the realm of what is left out of the mirror, the realm of "constraint and contingence" where human life is reduced to animal nature.[21] This nature is defined either as the nothing of brute physical nature, as it is most often with women, or as a subordinate social nature defined by those with power and imposed as the universal truth on those without power. In either case, God and his representatives relegate others to a realm of constraint and contingence.

For Marx, as for de Beauvoir, the human only becomes a subject by exercising the power to make human nature, by transcending through creative action the limits of biology or a given cultural arrangement. From the position of subject, man sees "no justification for present existence other than its expansion into an indefinitely open future."[22] A subject makes history and his or her own nature by making history. Man's religion robs this power from women and those men who are not God's representatives, from those who are not, at least yet, the same.

In de Beauvoir's view, man relegates woman to the realm of immanence by compelling "her to assume the status of Other." Men "propose to stabilize [woman] as an object and to doom her to immanence since her transcendence is to be overshadowed and forever transcended by another ego (*conscience*) which is essential and sovereign." [23] Marx said much the same about God and his representatives: They relegate other men to the realm of immanence. In religion, man's transcendence is overshadowed and forever transcended by another ego, that of God, which is taken to be sovereign. Men's freedom or transcendence is also overshadowed by those select men who represent God and claim, like kings and priests, as their sole right earthly sovereignty. Moreover, Marx, in contrast to Fichte, saw that man's freedom was overshadowed by those philosophers who claimed as theirs the right to define universal truth and the laws of nature. He saw that these men, like men of religion, use ideological power to liberate the people by constraint.

For Marx, the criticism of religion as well as the ideology that functioned like it was a correlate of revolution.[24] Simply put, men would come out of their stupor and realize that God and his representatives were really men. When men wake up and recognize the God in the mirror as nothing other than themselves, they are freed from the crippling religious and philosophical ideologies that convince him that others, and ultimately God as the absolutely other, possess what they lack—the power to shape history and their own nature. When man stops projecting himself as the inessential other of God the essential subject and God's representatives, he is freed. Criticizing religion empowers him to see himself for what he really is and to reclaim his own powers stolen from him by his divinizing mirror.

What happens to woman when man wakes up? Man's criticism of his religion may enable her to understand his religion and his philosophies as ideological, but does it free her from her place as his inessential other? De Beauvoir pointed out that it has always been males who have looked into the divinizing mirror of religion and that women "have no religion or poetry of their own: They still dream through the dreams of men. Gods made by males are the gods [women] worship." [25] These gods are projections of male imagination and actors in "virile myths," reflecting man's essential qualities, his powers to shape his own world and destiny, to be a subject of history. Because "women do not set themselves up as Subject," they have "erected no virile myth in which their projects are reflected." Because "representation of the world, like the world itself, is the work of men," women have no religion of their own.[26]

De Beauvoir recognized that men have at times seen a female God in the mirror, most often in the form of a mother. Thinking about Pestalozzi and Novalis, we might say that at times in man's individual and collective nursery woman's image eclipsed his own in his divine mirror and he mistook it, at least briefly, for his own. As Fichte feared, man then confuses the mother's body with his own and that leads him into confusion about his essential human qualities, his mind and will. But with the help of experts in religion and philosophy, this confusion is short-lived.

De Beauvoir explained that the images of female gods have only been fleeting because they reflect too much of what man sees as inessential and animallike. "To glorify the mother," she wrote, "is to accept birth, life, and death under their animal and humanly social forms at once, it is to proclaim the harmony of nature and society." [27] Except in the highly unusual religious vision of the female God in Novalis, in which creative fluids of nature abound, to proclaim the harmony of nature and society is to affirm the status quo, that is, to "naturalize" a given state of society, and thus to freeze history.

When men see God as a female in the mirror, they

are repulsed because she reflects not their powers of transcendence but the threat of immanence, the threat of having a fixed biological nature that condemns them to existence in the clutches of a fixed natural world. When
men see God as a female in the mirror, she does not
look the same.

In describing woman's dilemma as man's other,
de Beauvoir wrote, "The drama of woman lies in this
conflict between the fundamental aspirations of every
subject (ego)—who always regards the self as the essential—and the compulsions of a situation in which she is
the inessential." [28] Woman's task of liberation is to lay
claim, alongside man and reciprocally with him, to the
position of subject and to enter into the projects of transcendence. It would seem then that insofar as modern
Western man's criticism of his God makes way for oppressed men to claim the position of subject, it could do
the same for women. To put this simply, woman should
be well rid of religion. Any turn to religion, any invitation to explore regions of spirituality, would seem to be
a reactionary move and an abandonment of perhaps the
most liberating modern Western theory.

But contemporary women-centered feminists refuse
to relinquish religion to modern man's critique. In one
sense they are saying that when woman wakes up to the
truth that God is really man, nothing happens. She is
not empowered by any flash of self-recognition because
she was never looking at or misidentifying her own image in the mirror in the first place. She was always seeing
the male's self-reflection. She was never in the circle of
reflection, neither in the illusion nor in the reality.

These women are now demanding their own divinizing mirror with which to create their own religion,
because they reject the contrast Marx and others have
drawn between religion as ideology and man's true and
purportedly scientific knowledge of his actual conditions
and potentials brought about by his awakening. Women

are refusing to accept the social and political dynamic of religion as one that always serves the interests of the dominant group and causes a misidentification of human potential.

THE CRISIS IN THE WEST

Reflecting on the current women-centered exaltation of what we have called the feminine soul, the French feminist Julia Kristeva says that now the woman's movement is not only active at the sociopolitical level of culture but "situated within the very framework of the religious crisis of our civilization." [29] This is the crisis precipitated by those men, following Marx and Freud, who are trying to live without religion, without a god, without any illusions that there are powers beyond their control. Kristeva conjectures that the images of woman that feminists are worshiping as the representation of their powers are a "representation which makes up for the frustration imposed on women by the anterior code." [30] She identifies this code as that of Christianity *and* of those secular systems of thought that are merely its "lay humanist variant." [31] Our modern Western liberating humanist traditions repeat the story of the rule of the father and of the power of the one will and thought to create the world. Out of frustration, women, in what may seem an anachronistic and apolitical move in this postreligious age, are creating their own religious representations in their own divinizing mirror.

By seizing their own divinizing mirror, women-centered feminists hope to take control of the ideology of the feminine soul. But in reaching for religion they are not naive about ideology, its illusory quality or its material effects. In rejecting modern man's criticism of religion, the women-centered feminists are not claiming to go beyond ideology to absolute truth or to a value-free standpoint. We might say that they know they are in front of a mirror; they know they are creating an ideology. But they know too that it can have material effects.

These feminists are saying that if Western woman, along with man, gave up a divinizing mirror, she would be left with man's science. She would be left hoping that someday she would be an equal partner in his projects of transcendence. Rejecting religion and all illusory projections, including the illusion of a feminine soul, in order to take her place as a subject of history, woman should undergo a struggle for liberating knowledge similar to his. She should aspire, as de Beauvoir said, to man's project of transcendence, a project that only became possible for all men when modern men denied the reality of God and the privilege of all his earthly representatives.

But women-centered feminists do not want to be left with man's science or his secular project of transcendence. They, seemingly like the theologians of old, are saying that man really does have an absolute other. To put this simply, these feminists are saying that the true absolute other of man was never reflected in his divinizing mirror. When man woke up and realized that his God was nothing other than himself, he still did not appropriate as his own what he left out of the mirror. Outside the male ego and its reflected God is a reality that never entered his circle of reflection.

Certainly, just when Western women are beginning in ever-increasing numbers to act out de Beauvoir's mandate that they become subjects of history and assume their own projects of transcendence in mutual reciprocity with men, the embrace of religion and the feminine soul may seem a reactionary move. But it is rather an act of desperation arising from the horror of the order of death men have created in the name of secular transcendence. Sharon Welch describes vividly the effects of death that have been the consequence of modern man's illusion-free science: "The twentieth century is the denouement of the [modern] Western ideal of civilization. We stand on the brink of extinction through nuclear holocaust or ecological disaster, a species whose greatest achievement in this last century has been the perfection of the art of genocide. From the first bombings of civilian targets by the fascists in the Spanish Civil War, through the British and American strategic bombing of Germany, through Hitler's death camps and the genocidal warfare of the United States against the people of Vietnam, to our current flirtation with limited nuclear war, the [age of self-determining man] has distinguished itself by folly and cruelty." [32]

These are the realities of man's illusion-free science that affect the bodies of women who have been the vehicles of the biopolitics of modern genocidal man. These are the realities that engender the psychological conflicts of women who have achieved entry in the man's world on an "equal" footing. And these are the realities that make women reach for the divinizing mirror. Not at home with their new identity as equals with men, unable to embrace the "old" and still available identity as his inessential other, women who have entered into the project of transcendence do not experience the joy of being free, autonomous subjects of history, but the pain of being split, divided subjects.

Claudine Hermann says it simply: "If woman remains true to herself, and continues to think in terms of harmony rather than struggle, of giving rather than exchange, she will be ruthlessly crushed [in a man's world]. . . . What she gains in the social arena she will lose on a personal level. It means nothing to allow women to participate in society if it robs them of everything that makes them different." [33]

The terrifying domination characterizing the age of man's maturity motivates women to reach for the divinizing mirror. What they hope to discover by looking into it is not merely the virtues of nurture and intimacy as the necessary complements to man's ethics of transcendence and his definitions of justice and equality but a completely new, transformative ethic.

WOMEN IN THEIR DIVINIZING MIRROR

If the God of Western religion and metaphysics is man's illusion and disappeared when man matured to take control of history and nature, what kind of God can appear to check the death-dealing effects of that control? What does woman see in the mirror? It is too early to answer in detail, but tentative descriptions can be given.

Woman sees, as Rich says, a multipleasured body, a reproductive body, a body in continuity with nature, a body out of which women express their genius or soul. Most importantly, what she sees does not remain static or one.

Like man, woman sees her essential qualities in the mirror, but unlike him she does not see these together with a single part of the body that has been spiritualized and cut off from matter and physical nature. In describing the essential qualities of women, Cixous writes, "If there is a 'propriety of woman,' it is paradoxically her capacity to depropriate unselfishly, body without end, without appendage, without principal 'parts.' If she is a whole, it's a whole composed of parts that are wholes, not simple partial objects but a moving, limitlessly changing ensemble, a cosmos tirelessly traversed by Eros, an immense astral space not organized around any one sun that's any more of a star than others." [34]

Woman does not separate her physical parts from her thought and will, because she images her body and her creativity in continuity with nature.[35] Woman sees her her own fluid body as the source of words or signs that continually open up the parameters of what can be thought: "Text: my body—shot through with streams of song; I don't mean the overbearing, clutchy 'mother' but, rather, what touches you, that equivoice that affects you, fills your breast with an urge to come to language and launches your force; the rhythm that laughs you; the intimate recipient who makes all metaphors possible and desirable; body (body? bodies?), no more describable than god, the soul, or the Other; that part of you that leaves a space between yourself and urges you to inscribe in language your woman's style." [36]

Of course, woman sees the mother in her divinizing mirror. In fact, she sees something very like the mother Fichte feared, the loving mother who disrupts the word and laws of the father: "In women there is always more or less of the mother who makes everything all right, who nourishes, and who stands up against separation; a force that will not be cut off but will knock the wind out of the codes." [37]

And, finally, what she does not see is one. Irigaray writes, "For all that, she does not constitute a *one*. She is not locked into or onto one truth or one essence. The essence of a truth remains foreign to her. She neither has nor is a being. She does not set up a feminine truth in opposition to masculine truth. Which would amount to playing the castration game—where the male is the castrated one." Somewhat like Daly, Irigaray identifies the divinized image of women as a becoming that resists any fixed being and thus any fixed and hierarchical opposition between people. In a passage that calls to mind the endlessly responsive bodies and eternal births of Fable's tale, Irigaray writes, "If the female sex has its being in embracing, in endlessly sharing its lips, its boundaries, its limits and its 'contents,' in ceaselessly becoming the other, she has no stability of being. She has her being in opening a relation with the other whom she does not take into herself, like a pelican, but to whom she eternally gives birth." [38]

Whatever else, this fluid and unstable divinized image of woman in the mirror reflects an ever-present differentiating. This is because what is there "in the beginning," the finite body and the nature to which it is bound, stays in the mirror. The making of this God thus does not involve a differentiation that is hierarchical. There are no essential qualities separated out and raised in front of the mirror, and no inessential qualities lowered beneath the mirror. In other words, the imaging of this

God does not necessitate the identification of another that is not the one.

For this reason, there is hope that the imaging of this God will not lead to the oppression men experienced when they lost the sense of identity with their God in the mirror. There is, in a sense, nothing inessential to turn to. Moreover, as we have seen, women already know that they are standing in front of a mirror. They are consciously doing this in order to be empowered.

Julia Kristeva identifies the most crucial promise of woman's divine image: its potential to support the creation of a society in which there is no need for a scapegoat, for a rejected object. If woman's divine image does not entail the separation of an inessential other, if women resist the temptation to purify in their religion and refuse to project all evil onto men or any other group, then their image is one of a new and finally mature human. It is perhaps an image that will allow women and men to accept "the potentialities of *victim/executioneer* which characterize each identity, each subject, each sex." [39] Perhaps it will allow for difference without domination.

In *Of Woman Born,* Rich describes the problem of infanticide in eighteenth-century Germany and its relation to Goethe's praise of the eternal feminine, and then turns to the act of Joanne Michulski, a suburban Chicago housewife and mother of eight, who in 1974 decapitated her two youngest children on her front lawn. In order to recover Michulski's story and the conditions that drove her several times to a bed of depression and madness, Rich must interpret the newspaper accounts that sensationalized her as a bad mother. These stories make this woman a scapegoat, "an escape valve; through her the passions and the blind raging waters of a suppressed knowledge are permitted to churn their way so that they need not emerge in less extreme situations as lucid rebellion." [40] The scapegoat is necessary to localize and set apart the many mundane violences that press on and emerge from each self-identity, each sex, each structure of human society, and allow the knowledge of the true origins of violence to be suppressed. For example, when women read about Joan Michulski, says Rich, they are supposed to see her as the antithesis of their own identities as good mothers and respond by resolving "to become better, more patient, more long-suffering, to cling to what passes for sanity." [41] What passes for sanity means conforming to the laws and ideologies of those who have been privileged to define the order of the good society and of the good mother.

Naive belief in the truth of post-Reformation Western ideology of the good mother or of the morally superior feminine soul is not an option for women. We must not forget the reality of maternal infanticide as a part of history nor deny the potential of an impulse to infanticide that arises from a fettered body. On the contrary, women need to dare to be mad, to dream, to envision the soul that might emerge from a free body. We need to speak and write the words that knock the winds out of the codes of the good society that have restrained us. To empower ourselves we need to use our own divinizing mirror that reflects our truth as "ultimate." But if, like the men before us, we see only a partial image in the mirror, if all we allow ourselves to see is the good mother, we will find no more than an abstract and potentially violent ideal.

If we do not split off part of ourselves, if we do not forget that we are split ourselves, perhaps our image can elicit an ethic that allows for a responsibility that is not only caring, as Gilligan proposes, but also deeply and radically political. Perhaps we can discover a responsibility that looks in all directions for its victims and not just at some abstract ideal of right and good that allows us to identify a scapegoat.

If the new divine image of women, in refusing the logic of identity, leaves no room for a scapegoat, then, as Cixous claims, we will know that "all the stories would have to be told differently"—both the old religious story and its lay humanist variant. Then "the future would be incalculable, the historical forces would, will, change hands, bodies." Then "another thinking as yet not thinkable will transform the functioning of all society." [42]

If we in the West insist on defending life by the logic and weapons of death, our future is all too calculable. We desperately need the different voices, other visions, and the invitation to imagine offered us by the women-centered feminists.

Notes
Selected Bibliography
Index

Notes

Preface

1. G. W. F. Hegel, *Phenomenology of Spirit,* translated by A. V. Miller (Oxford: Oxford University Press, 1977), p. 288.

Chapter 1. Rebirth of the Feminine Soul

1. Jean Isoulet, *La Cité Moderne, metaphysique de la sociologie.* Quoted in Viola Klein, *The Feminine Character: History of an Ideology* (London: Kegan Paul, Trench, Trubner, 1946), p. 167.
2. H. Caffarel, ed., *Marriage Is Holy,* translated by Bernard G. Murchland, C.S.C. (Notre Dame, Ind.: Fides Publishers Association, 1957), p. 79.
3. Adrienne Rich, *Of Woman Born: Motherhood as Experience and Institution* (New York: A Bantam Book, 1977), p. 292.
4. Sheila Rowbotham, *Women, Resistance, and Revolution: A History of Women and Revolution in the Modern World* (New York: Vintage Books, 1974), pp. 38–39.
5. See Eli Zaretsky, "Capitalism, the Family, and Personal Life," *Socialist Revolution* 13–14 (January–April 1973), p. 114.
6. Caffarel, ed., *Marriage Is Holy,* p. 68.
7. Ibid., pp. 70, 78.
8. Ibid., p. 78.
9. Ibid., pp. 77–78.
10. Ibid., p. 69.
11. Ibid., p. 82.
12. Ibid., pp. 71–72.
13. Ibid., p. 106.
14. Karl Marx, "A Contribution to the Critique of Hegel's 'Philosophy of Right,' " in *Critique of Hegel's "Philosophy of Right,"* translated by Annette Jolin and Joseph O'Malley and edited and introduced by Joseph O'Malley (Cambridge: Cambridge University Press, 1970), p. 131.
15. See Christopher Lasch, *Haven in a Heartless World: The Family Besieged* (New York: Basic Books, 1979).

16. See Rich, *Of Woman Born*, p. 292.
17. Carol Gilligan, *In a Different Voice: Psychological Theory and Women's Development* (Cambridge, Mass.: Harvard University Press, 1982).
18. Gilligan, *In a Different Voice*, p. 172.
19. Donna Stanton, "Language and Revolution: The Franco-American Dis-Connection," in *The Future of Difference*, edited by Hester Eisenstein and Alice Jardine (Boston: G. K. Hall, 1980), p. 78.
20. Caffarel, ed., *Marriage Is Holy*, p. 68.
21. Rich, *Of Woman Born*, p. 292.
22. Luce Irigaray, "This Sex Which Is Not One," *New French Feminisms: An Anthology*, edited by Elaine Marks and Isabelle de Courtivron (New York: Schocken Books, 1981), p. 101. This book and *Signs* 7, 1 (Autumn 1981) provide good introductions to French feminism. Julia Kristeva's *Desire in Language: A Semiotic Approach to Literature and Art*, edited by Leon S. Roudiez and translated by Thomas Gora, Alice Jardine, and Leon S. Roudiez (New York: Columbia University Press, 1982), has been especially important for my own work.
23. Stanton, "Language and Revolution," p. 78.
24. Mary Daly, *Pure Lust: Elemental Feminist Philosophy* (Boston: Beacon Press, 1984), p. 397.
25. See Simone de Beauvoir, *The Second Sex*, translated and edited by H. M. Parshley (New York: Vintage Books, 1974), pp. 3–69.
26. Among those who have employed Marxist and Freudian thought for gender analysis toward liberation are Nancy Chodorow, *The Reproduction of Mothering: Psychoanalysis and the Sociology of Gender* (Berkeley and Los Angeles: University of California Press, 1978); Ann Foreman, *Femininity as Alienation: Women and the Family in Marxism and Psychoanalysis* (London: Pluto Press, 1977); Annette Kuhn and AnnMarie Wolpe, *Feminism and Materialism: Women and Modes of Production* (London: Routledge and Kegan Paul, 1978); Juliet Mitchell, *Psychoanalysis and Feminism* (New York: Vintage Books, 1975); Sheila Rowbotham, *Woman's Consciousness, Man's World* (Harmondsworth, Middlesex, England: Penguin Books, 1973).
27. Karl Marx, "A Contribution to the Critique of Hegel's 'Philosophy of Right,'" pp. 131–132.
28. Hester Eisenstein, *Contemporary Feminist Thought* (Boston: G. K. Hall, 1983), p. xv.
29. Ibid., p. 135.

30. Hilary Rose, "Hand, Brain, and Heart: A Feminist Epistemology for the Natural Sciences," *Signs* 9, 1 (Autumn 1983): 83.
31. Ibid. See Mary O'Brien, *The Politics of Reproduction* (Boston, London, and Henley: Routledge and Kegan Paul, 1981), for an exposition on reproductive consciousness, esp. pp. 19–64.
32. Ibid., p. 82.
33. Karl Marx, *Capital*, vol. 1 (New York: International Publishers, 1967), p. 177.
34. Isaac D. Balbus, *Marxism and Domination: A Neo-Hegelian, Feminist, Psychoanalytic Theory of Sexual, Political, and Technological Liberation* (Princeton: Princeton University Press, 1982), p. 76.
35: Sigmund Freud, *An Outline of Psycho-Analysis*, translated and edited by James Strachey (New York: W. W. Norton, 1949), p. 45.
36. Ibid.
37. Ibid.
38. Ibid., p. 46.
39. Ibid., p. 47.
40. Balbus, *Marxism and Domination*, p. 174.
41. Freud, *An Outline of Psycho-Analysis*, p. 50.
42. Ibid., pp. 50–51.
43. Rich, *Of Woman Born*, p. 196.
44. See Chodorow, *The Reproduction of Mothering*.
45. Rich, *Of Woman Born*, p. 197.
46. Ibid., p. 290.
47. Eisenstein, *Contemporary Feminist Thought*, p. 145.
48. Ibid., pp. 144–145.
49. Ibid., p. 145.
50. Marx, *Critique of Hegel's "Philosophy of Right,"* pp. 24, 27, 29. See also Marilyn Chapin Massey, *Christ Unmasked: The Meaning of "The Life of Jesus" in German Politics* (Chapel Hill: University of North Carolina Press, 1983), pp. 81–112.
51. Sigmund Freud, *Totem and Taboo*, translated and edited by James Strachey (New York: W. W. Norton, 1950).
52. Mary Daly, *Beyond God the Father: Toward a Philosophy of Women's Liberation* (Boston: Beacon Press, 1973), p. 77.
53. Among these exposures are Sheila D. Collins, *A Different Heaven and Earth: A Feminist Perspective on Religion* (Valley Forge, Penn.: Judson Press, 1974); Mary Daly, *Beyond God the Father; Toward a Philosophy of Women's Liberation* (Boston: Beacon Press, 1973), and *Gyn/Ecology:*

The Metaethics of a Radical Feminism (Boston: Beacon Press, 1978); Rosemary Radford Ruether, *New Woman, New Earth: Sexist Ideologies and Human Liberation* (New York: Seabury Press, 1975), and *Sexism and God-Talk: Toward a Feminist Theology* (Boston: Beacon Press, 1983); Peggy Reeves Sanday, *Female Power and Male Dominance: On the Origins of Sexual Inequality* (Cambridge: Cambridge University Press, 1981).

54. Novalis, *Schriften*, 2 vols., edited by Paul Kluckhohn and Richard Samuel (Leipzig: Bibliographisches Institut, A.G., 1929), vol. 2, 29–30.

55. Some of the earliest research on the mother-goddess traditions includes J. J. Bachofen, *Myth, Religion, and Mother Right* (1861); C. G. Jung, *Symbols of Transformation* (1912); Robert Briffault, *The Mothers* (1927). More recent studies include Erich Neumann, *The Great Mother: An Analysis of the Archetype*, translated by Ralph Manheim, Bollingen Series vol. 47 (Princeton: Princeton University Press, 1955); E. O. James, *The Cult of the Mother Goddess* (New York: Praeger, 1959); Raphael Patai, *The Hebrew Goddess* (New York: Avon Books, 1967). Merlin Stone, in *When God Was a Woman* (New York: Harcourt Brace Jovanovich, 1976), tells the story of goddess worship and documents the patriarchal reimaging, and subsequent suppression, of the goddess. The anthropological essays in *Mother Worship: Theme and Variations*, edited by James J. Preston (Chapel Hill: University of North Carolina Press, 1982), explore varieties of devotion to the sacred mother still practiced today.

56. I have borrowed this term from Michel Foucault, whose histories of our modern Western philosophical and political discourses have influenced this study. Foucault views sets of ideas as arising from and having social effects within a network of specific or, as he calls them, local exercises of social, political, and economic power. His historical perspective differs from that of intellectual historians who trace the similarity and differences of sets of ideas over long periods of time and thus, of necessity, abstract them from their immediate sociopolitical context of genesis and social influences (i.e., a history of ideas about the unique qualities of women's interiority in the political philosophy of the eighteenth, nineteenth, and twentieth centuries). It also differs from the perspective of social historians who relate the origin and influence of ideas to macrosocial or economic power relations (i.e., a history of

the relation of ideas about women's unique spiritual nature to the economic conditions of bourgeois society). Although these more customary historical perspectives are fruitful and will be used here, they miss the historically concrete power relations involved in the production and social influence of sets of ideas in the past, and they fail to suggest the subtle and pervasive social influence of the heritage of these ideas in the present. In this study, I will do something Foucault does not do. I will identify the discourse on the feminine soul as a specific type of modern discourse that was essential to the formation of the modern Western discourse of political theory.

57. Rich, *Of Woman Born*, pp. 264–265.
58. Rose, "Hand, Brain, and Heart," p. 83.
59. In *Discipline and Punish: The Birth of the Prison*, translated by Alan Sheridan (New York: Vintage Books, 1979), Michel Foucault claims that there is a modern type of soul that is not the "reactivated remnants of an [out-grown religious] ideology" (p. 29). He defines this post-Christian, postreligious soul as the correlate of modern mechanisms of social control and he claims that it is possessed by all those, female and male, who are disciplined for subservience in contemporary society. Foucault defines this soul as a "reality referent" upon which various "concepts have been constructed and domains of analysis carved out: psyche, subjectivity, personality, consciousness" (pp. 29–30). On these regions of human interiority "have been built scientific techniques and discourses, and the moral claims of humanism" (pp. 29–30). Foucault further explains, this modern type of soul is a "real, noncorporal" element "in which are articulated the effects of a certain type of power ... [and this soul is] the referent of a certain type of knowledge, it is that machinery by which power relations give rise to a possible corpus of knowledge, and knowledge extends and reinforces the effects of this power" (p. 29). The clearest example of the type of relationship between knowledge about the modern feminine soul and social power described by Foucault is that relationship, of paramount concern to feminists today, between the bodies of scientific knowledge about women's unique psychological capacities for parenting and the vast range of social and economic policies aimed at securing women's "freedom" to exercise these capacities.
60. Biddy Martin, "Feminism, Criticism, and Foucault," *New German Critique* 27 (Fall 1982): 3. Martin thinks, as I do,

that some of the insights of Foucault can be most helpful to feminists. Foucault views ideology, in the sense of sets of ideas, not as mere mental epiphenomenon of specific economic and social conditions, as a simplified Marxism would have it, but rather as possessing themselves a material power by which they can function as instruments of social normalization. Another way to put this is to say that sets of ideas are interwoven in such complex ways throughout the fabric of a culture that they cannot be reduced to an economic or even any simple social base. It is also to say that ideas that are granted the status of scientific truth have a particular access to material power because they spread readily through many institutions and social practices and thus affect behavior through multiple channels.

61. Stanton, "Language and Revolution," p. 78.

Chapter 2. Biopolitics and the Birth of the Feminine Soul

1. Johann Heinrich Pestalozzi, "Ueber Gesetzgebung und Kindermord" (1793). Cited in Oscar Helmuth Werner, *The Unmarried Mother in German Literature, with Special Reference to the Period 1770–1800* (New York: Columbia University Press, 1917), p. 7.
2. Foucault, *Discipline and Punish*, p. 30.
3. Interview with Simone de Beauvoir, in *New French Feminisms*, edited by Elaine Marks and Isabelle de Courtivron, p. 153.
4. de Beauvoir, *The Second Sex*, p. 168.
5. Rich, *Of Woman Born*, pp. 264–265.
6. Werner, *The Unmarried Woman*, p. 7.
7. Ibid., p. 10.
8. Ibid., pp. 35–36.
9. Ibid., p. 35.
10. Ibid., p. 36 (my emphasis).
11. Ibid.
12. Ibid., p. 37.
13. Mary Lindemann, "Love for Hire: The Regulation of the Wet-Nursing Business in Eighteenth-Century Hamburg," *Journal of Family History* 6 (Winter 1981): 380. Cited from Johann Peter Frank, *System of a Complete Medical Police* (1780), pp. 373–380.
14. Jean-Jacques Rousseau, *Emile* (1762). Cited in Susan Moller Okin, *Women in Western Political Thought* (Princeton: Princeton University Press, 1979), p. 191.

15. Lindemann, "Love for Hire," p. 391. Cited from Frank, *System of a Complete Medical Police*, pp. 421, 419.
16. Lindemann, "Love for Hire," p. 391; *System of a Complete Medical Police*, pp. 421, 419.
17. Lindemann, "Love for Hire," p. 391; *System of a Complete Medical Police*, p. 417.
18. From the Prussian "Allgemeines Landrecht." Cited in *Women, the Family and Freedom: The Debate in Documents*, vol. 1, edited by Susan Groag Bell and Karen M. Offen (Stanford, Calif.: Stanford University Press, 1983), p. 39.
19. Lindemann, "Love for Hire," p. 380.
20. Ibid., p. 383.
21. Ibid.
22. Werner, *The Unmarried Mother*, p. 56.
23. Karin Hausen, "Family and Role Division: The Polarization of Sexual Stereotypes in the Nineteenth Century—An Aspect of the Dissociation of Work and Family Life," in *The German Family*, edited by Richard J. Evans and W. R. Lee (London: Croom Helm, 1981), p. 57, n. 16.
24. Ibid., p. 57, n. 16.
25. Ibid., pp. 54–55, n. 5.
26. Ibid., p. 57.
27. Foucault, *Discipline and Punish*, p. 50.
28. Ibid., p. 102.
29. Ibid., pp. 102–103.
30. Marx, "A Contribution to the Critique of Hegel's Philosophy of Right," p. 138.
31. Hausen, "Family and Role Division," p. 57.
32. Julius Hoffmann, *Die "Hausvaterliteratur" und die "Predigten über den christlichen Hausstand"* (Berlin: Verlag Julius Beltz, 1959), p. 92.
33. Ibid., p. 105.
34. Ibid., p. 101.
35. Ibid., p. 97.
36. Ibid., p. 115.
37. Ibid.
38. Ibid., p. 116.
39. Ibid., pp. 117, 123.
40. Steven Ozment, *When Fathers Ruled: Family Life in Reformation Europe* (Cambridge, Mass.: Harvard University Press, 1983), p. 57.
41. Hoffmann, *Die "Hausvaterliteratur,"* pp. 123–131.
42. Ibid., p. 129.
43. Ibid., p. 128.

44. Ozment, *When Fathers Ruled,* p. 65.
45. Ibid., p. 65, n. 56.
46. See Daly, *Gyn/Ecology,* pp. 114–115.
47. Ibid., p. 122.
48. Ozment, *When Fathers Ruled,* p. 147.
49. Hoffmann, *Die "Hausvaterliteratur,"* p. 135.

Chapter 3. The Feminine Soul in Leonard and Gertrude

1. Johann Heinrich Pestalozzi, *Leonard and Gertrude,* translated by Eva Channing (Boston: D. C. Heath, 1885), p. 94. Pestalozzi kept expanding and editing *Leonard and Gertrude* for over forty years. In its full length the book fills five volumes. The early German editions are *Lienhard und Gertrud. Ein Buch für das Volk,* 4 vols. (Stuttgart: J. G. Cotta, 1819–1820); L. W. Seyffart, ed., 5 vols. (Brandenburg: H. A. Müller, 1869–1870).
2. Karl Marx, *Writings of the Young Marx on Philosophy and Society,* edited and translated by Lloyd D. Easton and Kurt H. Guddat (Garden City, N.Y.: Doubleday, Anchor, 1967), p. 409.
3. Rose, "Hand, Brain, and Heart," p. 83.
4. Werner, *The Unmarried Mother,* p. 4.
5. Ibid.
6. Kate Silber, *Pestalozzi: The Man and His Work* (London: Routledge and Kegan Paul, 1960), p. 53.
7. Ibid., pp. 55–56.
8. Pestalozzi, *Leonard and Gertrude,* pp. 3, 5.
9. Ibid., p. 67.
10. Ibid., p. 72.
11. Ibid.
12. Ibid., p. 82. In later editions, Pestalozzi deleted the scene of even this mock execution because it violated his readers' sensibilities.
13. Ibid., p. 72.
14. Ibid., p. 82.
15. Foucault, *Discipline and Punish,* pp. 102–103.
16. Pestalozzi, *Leonard and Gertrude,* p. 94.
17. Ibid.
18. Ibid.
19. Ibid., p. 95.
20. Ibid., p. 84.
21. Ibid., p. 95.
22. Ibid., p. 85.
23. Ibid.

24. Ibid., p. 86.
25. Ibid.
26. Ibid., p. 85.
27. Ibid., p. 86.
28. Ibid., p. 94.
29. Ibid., p. 85.
30. Ibid., p. 87.
31. Ibid., p. 135.
32. Ibid., p. 157.
33. Ibid.
34. Ibid.
35. Ibid.
36. Ibid., p. 156.
37. Ibid.
38. Ibid.
39. Ibid., p. 135.
40. Ibid.

Chapter 4. Divinization and Suppression of Gertude's Soul

1. Sigmund Freud, *Civilization and Its Discontents,* translated and edited by James Strachey (New York and London: W. W. Norton, 1961), p. 56.
2. Gilligan, *In a Different Voice,* p. 98.
3. Johann Gottlieb Fichte, *Addresses to the German Nation,* translated by R. F. Jones and G. H. Turnball (Chicago and London: Open Court Publishing Company, 1922), pp. 172–173. This translation is based on Vogt's edition of Fichte's *Reden an die deutsche Nation* in the Bibliothek pädagogischer Klassiker, Langensalza, 1896.
4. Johann Heinrich Pestalozzi, *How Gertrude Teaches Her Children: An Attempt to Help Mothers to Teach Their Own Children and an Account of the Method,* translated by Lucy E. Holland and Francis Turner and edited with introduction and notes by Ebenezer Cooke, 5th ed. (London: George Allen and Unwin; Syracuse, N.Y.: C. W. Bardeen, 1915), pp. 194–195. The work was first published in 1894.
5. Ibid., p. 127.
6. Ibid.
7. Ibid., pp. 127–128.
8. Ibid., p. 128.
9. Ibid.
10. Ibid.

11. Ibid.
12. Ibid., p. 129.
13. Marx, "A Contribution to the Critique of Hegel's 'Philosophy of Right,'" p. 138.
14. Ibid.
15. Ibid.
16. Ibid.
17. Ibid., p. 142.
18. Gilligan, *In a Different Voice*, p. 98.
19. Ibid., p. 173.
20. Pestalozzi, *How Gertrude Teaches Her Children*, p. 197.
21. Ibid., p. 182. In describing children, both Pestalozzi and Froebel use male pronouns. I have kept these pronouns in the translations. I have also kept them in my commentary where they are intended to signify a male child.
22. Ibid., p. 75.
23. Ibid., p. 182.
24. Ibid., pp. 182–183.
25. Ibid., p. 183.
26. Ibid., pp. 183–184.
27. Ibid., p. 184.
28. Ibid., p. 183.
29. Ibid., p. 184.
30. Ibid.
31. Ibid., pp. 184–185.
32. Ibid.
33. Ibid., p. 185.
34. Ibid., pp. 185–186.
35. Ibid., p. 186.
36. Ibid.
37. Ibid., pp. 189–190.
38. Ibid., p. 190.
39. Ibid., p. 195.
40. Ibid., pp. 194–195.
41. Rich, *Of Woman Born*, p. 197.
42. Fichte, *Addresses to the German Nation*, Introduction, p. xxi.
43. Ibid., p. 163.
44. Ibid., p. 158.
45. Ibid., p. 159.
46. See Silber, *Pestalozzi*, pp. 74–75, for a discussion of philosophers' reactions to *Leonard and Gertrude*.
47. Fichte, *Addresses to the German Nation*, p. 173. (author emphas.)
48. Ibid., pp. 163–164.

49. de Beauvoir, *The Second Sex*, p. 162, n. 6.
50. Fichte, *Addresses to the German Nation*, p. 157.
51. Ibid., p. 158.
52. Ibid.
53. Ibid., p. 160.
54. Ibid.
55. Ibid., p. 20.
56. Ibid.
57. Ibid., p. 21.
58. Ibid., p. 22.
59. Ibid., p. 23.
60. Ibid., p. 22.
61. Ibid., p. 23.
62. Pestalozzi, *How Gertrude Teaches Her Children*, pp. 182–183.
63. Fichte, *Addresses to the German Nation*, p. 23.
64. Ibid.
65. Ibid., p. 24.
66. Ibid., p. 26.
67. Ibid., p. 25.
68. Ibid., p. 26.
69. Ibid.
70. Ibid., p. 163.
71. Ibid., p. 26.
72. Ibid., p. 28.
73. Ibid., p. 27.
74. Ibid., p. 161.
75. Ibid., p. 162.
76. Ibid., p. 163.
77. See Kristeva, *Desire in Language*.
78. Fichte, *Addresses to the German Nation*, pp. 162–163.
79. Ibid.
80. Ibid., p. 184.
81. Ibid., pp. 164–165.
82. Ibid., p. 164.
83. Ibid.
84. Ibid., p. 167.
85. Ibid., p. 172.
86. Ibid., p. 174.
87. Ibid., p. 172.
88. Ibid., pp. 172–173.
89. Ibid., p. 173.
90. Ibid.
91. Ibid., p. 178.
92. Ibid., p. 28.

Chapter 5. The Feminine Soul in Henry of Ofterdingen

1. Novalis, "Klingsohr's Tale," translated by Gordon Birrell, in *German Literary Fairy Tales*, edited by Frank G. Ryder and Robert M. Browning, The German Library, vol. 30 (New York: Continuum, 1983), p. 72.

2. Novalis, *Henry of Ofterdingen*, translated by Frederick S. Stallknecht (Cambridge: John Owen, 1842), p. 151. This translation is from the version of *Henry* in the five-volume collected works of Novalis edited by Ludwig Tieck and Friedrich Schlegel (Berlin, 1837–1846).

3. Freud, *Civilization and Its Discontents*, pp. 11–12.

4. Rowbotham, *Women, Resistance, and Revolution*, p. 38.

5. Cf. John Neubauer, *Novalis* (Boston: G. K. Hall, Twayne Publishers, 1980), pp. 126ff.

6. Novalis, *Henry*, p. 40.

7. Ibid., p. 26.

8. Ibid., pp. 127–128.

9. Ibid., p. 28.

10. Ibid., pp. 28–29.

11. Ibid., p. 29.

12. Ibid., p. 30.

13. Ibid.

14. Ibid., p. 151.

15. Ibid., p. 36.

16. Ibid., p. 37.

17. Ibid., p. 40.

18. Ibid., p. 41.

19. Ibid., pp. 28–29.

20. Ibid., pp. 51–52.

21. Ibid., p. 51.

22. Ibid., p. 49.

23. Ibid., p. 50.

24. Ibid.

25. Ibid., p. 51.

26. Ibid., p. 53.

27. Ibid., p. 55.

28. Ibid., p. 61.

29. Ibid.

30. Ibid., p. 68.

31. Ibid., pp. 69–70.

32. Ibid., p. 63.

33. Ibid., p. 74.

34. Ibid., p. 75.

35. Ibid., p. 76.

36. Ibid., p. 77.

37. Ibid., p. 79.
38. Ibid.
39. Ibid., p. 81.
40. Ibid.
41. Ibid.
42. Ibid., p. 83.
43. Ibid., p. 93.
44. Ibid., p. 92.
45. Ibid., p. 96.
46. Ibid., p. 111.
47. Ibid., p. 133.
48. Novalis, "Klingsohr's Tale," p. 52.
49. Ibid.
50. Ibid., p. 53.
51. Ibid.
52. Ibid., pp. 53–54.
53. Ibid., p. 55.
54. Ibid.
55. Ibid.
56. Ibid., p. 56.
57. Ibid., p. 57.
58. Ibid.
59. Ibid.
60. Ibid., p. 58.
61. Ibid., p. 60.
62. Ibid., p. 61.
63. Ibid.
64. Ibid.
65. Ibid., pp. 61–62.
66. Ibid., pp. 62–65.
67. Ibid., p. 66.
68. Ibid.
69. Ibid.
70. Ibid., p. 69.
71. Ibid., p. 70.
72. Ibid., pp. 70–71.
73. Ibid., p. 72.
74. Ibid.
75. Ibid.
76. Ibid., p. 73.
77. Ibid., p. 76.

Chapter 6. Domestication of Henry's Visions of the Feminine Soul

1. Franz Xaver von Baader, *Beiträge zur Elementar-phisio-logie*, in *Sämtliche Werke*, vol. 3 (Leipzig, 1850–1860); rpt.

Aalen, 1963), p. 226, as quoted in John Neubauer, *Bifocal Vision: Novalis' Philosophy of Nature and Disease* (Chapel Hill: University of North Carolina Press, 1971), p. 156, n. 20 (my translation).

2. Marx, *Capital*, p. 177.

3. Friedrich Schleiermacher, *Christmas Eve: Dialogue on the Incarnation*, translated, with introduction and notes, by Terrence N. Tice (Richmond, Va.: John Knox Press, 1967), p. 33. This is a translation of Schleiermacher's *Die Weihnachtsfeier: Ein Gespräch* (Berlin, 1826).

4. Novalis, *Henry*, p. 204.

5. Ibid.

6. Ibid., p. 206.

7. Ibid., p. 209.

8. Ibid., p. 210.

9. Ibid., p. 212.

10. Ibid.

11. Ibid., p. 228.

12. Novalis, "Klingsohr's Tale," p. 72.

13. Ibid., p. 73.

14. Novalis, as quoted in Neubauer, *Bifocal Vision*, p. 71.

15. Ibid.

16. See n. 1.

17. de Beauvoir, *The Second Sex*, p. 171.

18. Ibid., p. 170.

19. Ibid., p. 164; see also n. 3.

20. Ibid., p. 164.

21. Luce Irigaray, "This Sex Which Is Not One," p. 103.

22. Ibid.

23. Ibid.

24. Novalis, *Schriften*, eds., Paul Kluckhohn and Richard Samuel, 2nd edition (Stuttgart: Kohlhammer, 1960–1975), III, p. 283 as quoted in Neubauer, *Novalis*, p. 61.

25. Ibid., p. 54.

26. Ibid., p. 56.

27. Ibid., p. 61.

28. de Beauvoir, *The Second Sex*, p. 186.

29. Ibid.

30. Ibid., p. 194.

31. Ibid.

32. Schleiermacher, *Christmas Eve*, p. 32.

33. Ibid., p. 33.

34. Ibid., p. 32.

35. Ibid., p. 33.

36. Ibid.

37. Ibid., p. 34.
38. Ibid., p. 35.
39. Ibid., p. 36.
40. Ibid., p. 37.
41. Ibid.
42. Ibid.
43. Ibid., p. 48.
44. Ibid.
45. Ibid.
46. Ibid.
47. Ibid.
48. Ibid., p. 49.
49. Ibid.
50. Ibid.
51. See Hausen, "Family and Role Division," pp. 54–55.
52. Schleiermacher, *Christmas Eve*, p. 54.
53. Ibid.
54. Ibid.
55. Karl Barth responded to the feminine in Schleiermacher: "It is not the female-human which from its own standpoint is readier for God's work than the male-human.... Certainly the suggestion which Schleiermacher ventured to make in his Weihnachtsfeier... would have been better left unsaid." Barth, *Church Dogmatics*, vol. 1, 2, translated by G. T. Thomson and Harold Knight and edited by G. W. Bromiley and T. F. Torrance (Edinburgh: T. & T. Clark, 1956), p. 195. This is the authorized English translation from *Die kirchliche Dogmatik*, vol. 1, 2.

Chapter 7. The Domesticated Feminine Soul in Mother and Play Songs

1. Freud, *Civilization and Its Discontents*, p. 20.
2. Marx, *The German Ideology*, in *Writings of the Young Marx on Philosophy and Society*, p. 414.
3. Rich, *Of Woman Born*, p. 116.
4. Ibid.
5. Friedrich Fröbel, *Mutter- und Kose-Lieder: Dichtung und Bilder zur edlen Pflege des Kindheitlebens*, in *Pädagogische Schriften*, vol. 3, edited by Friedrich Seidel (Vienna and Leipzig: A. Pichler's Witwe and Sons, 1883). English translation: Friedrich Froebel, *The Mottoes and Commentaries of Friedrich Froebel's Mother Play*, translated and edited by Susan E. Blow (New York: D. Appleton,

1899). Blow undertook to clarify Froebel's style and thought and, as a result, her translation is a form of censorship. Here all translations are from the original German.

6. Gilligan, *In a Different Voice*, p. 172.
7. Fröbel, *Mutter- und Kose-Lieder*, pp. 155–156.
8. Ibid., p. 124.
9. Ibid., p. 153.
10. Ibid., p. 126.
11. Ibid.
12. Ibid., p. 121.
13. Ibid., p. 133.
14. Ibid., p. 127.
15. Ibid., p. 144.
16. Ibid., p. 126.
17. Ibid.
18. Ibid., p. 204.
19. Marx, *The German Ideology*, p. 414.
20. Fröbel, *Mutter- und Kose-Lieder*, pp. 200–201.
21. Ibid., p. 201.
22. Ibid., p. 202.
23. Rich, *Of Woman Born*, p. 81.
24. Ibid.
25. Robert B. Downs, *Friedrich Froebel* (Boston: G. K. Hall, 1978), p. 80.
26. B. von Marenholtz-Bülow, *Gesammelte Beiträge zum Verständiss der Fröbel'schen Erziehungidee*, 2 vols. (Kaffel: George H. Wigland, 1876–1877), vol. 1, p. 130.
27. Ibid.
28. Ibid.
29. Ibid., p. 4.
30. Daniel G. M. Schreber, *Kallipädie oder Erziehung zur Schönheit durch Naturgetreue und gleichmässige Förderung normaler Körperbildung* (Leipzig: Fleischer, 1858), p. 281. Cited in Morton Schatzman, *Soul Murder: Persecution in the Family* (London: Allen Lane, 1973), p. 16.
31. Schreber, *Kallipädie*, p. 136; Schatzman, *Soul Murder*, p. 21.
32. Daniel G. M. Schreber, *Kinaesiatrik oder die gymnastische Heilmethode. Für Ärzte und gebildete Nichtärzte nach eigenen Erfahrungen dargestellt* (1852), p. 35. Cited in Alfons Ritter, *Schreber, das Bildungssystem eines Arztes* (Inaugural Dissertation, Erlangen University, 1936), p. 66.
33. William H. Kilpatrick, *Froebel's Kindergarten Principles Critically Examined* (New York: Macmillan, 1916), p. 15.

Chapter 8. Religion, Gender, and Ideology:
A New Theory

1. Hélène Cixous, "The Newly Born Woman," in *New French Feminisms,* edited by Elaine Marks and Isabelle de Courtivron, pp. 96–97.
2. Rich, *Of Woman Born,* p. 292.
3. Hester Eisenstein, *Contemporary Feminist Thought,* p. 115.
4. Ibid., p. 145.
5. de Beauvoir, *The Second Sex,* p. 194.
6. Karl Marx and Friedrich Engels, *K. Marx and F. Engels on Religion* (Moscow: Foreign Languages Publishing House, 1957), p. 94.
7. Rich, *Of Woman Born,* p. 280.
8. Ibid., p. 281.
9. Ibid.
10. Ibid., p. 280.
11. Ibid.
12. Ibid., p. 180.
13. Ibid.
14. Biddy Martin, "Feminism, Criticism, and Foucault," p. 3.
15. Rich, *Of Woman Born,* p. 290.
16. On the relation of power and knowledge see the works of Michel Foucault.
17. de Beauvoir, *The Second Sex,* p. xviii.
18. Ibid.
19. I have formulated this description in my own way. Marx and, to a lesser extent, Freud were influenced by Ludwig Feuerbach's description of religion as projection. I have used that description as a basis here, but I have gone farther, using themes from the work of Michel Foucault and the French feminists.
20. The work of Jacques Derrida on the concept of the logos in Western philosophy and religion is relevant here. See *Dissemination,* translated by Barbara Johnson (Chicago: University of Chicago Press, 1981) and *Of Grammatology,* translated by Gayatri Chakravorty Spivak (Baltimore: Johns Hopkins University Press, 1976).
21. de Beauvoir, *The Second Sex,* p. xxxiii.
22. Ibid.
23. Ibid., pp. xxxiii–xxxiv.
24. Marx thought that the event of men's waking up to the truth of religion, which is their recognition of their own powers, was dependent upon the deterioration of economic and social conditions.

25. de Beauvoir, *The Second Sex,* p. 161.
26. Ibid.
27. Ibid., p. 196.
28. Ibid., p. xxxiv.
29. Julia Kristeva, "Women's Times," *Signs* 7, 1 (Autumn 1981): 32.
30. Ibid.
31. Ibid.
32. Sharon D. Welch, "The Battle for Truth: Foucault, Liberation Theology and the Insurrection of Subjugated Knowledges" (Ph.D. diss., Vanderbilt University, 1982), p. 297.
33. Claudine Herrmann, "The Virile System," in *New French Feminisms,* edited by Elaine Marks and Isabelle de Courtivron, pp. 88–89.
34. Hélène Cixous, "The Laugh of the Medusa," in *New French Feminisms,* edited by Elaine Marks and Isabelle de Courtivron, p. 259.
35. Ibid., p. 260.
36. Ibid., p. 252.
37. Ibid.
38. Luce Irigaray, *Amante marine de Friedrich Nietzsche* (Paris: Editions de Minuit, 1980), p. 92. Translated by Lillian S. Robinson in Christian Faure, "Twilight of the Goddesses," *Signs* 7, 1 (Autumn 1981): 85.
40. Rich, *Of Woman Born,* p. 283.
41. Ibid.
42. Hélène Cixous, "The Newly Born Woman," p. 93.

Selected Bibliography

Bachofen, J. J. *Myth, Religion and Mother Right: Selected Writings of Johann Jakob Bachofen*. Translated by Ralph Manheim. Princeton: Princeton University Press, 1967. Originally published in 1861.

Balbus, Isaac D. *Marxism and Domination: A Neo-Hegelian, Feminist, Psychoanalytic Theory of Sexual, Political, and Technological Liberation*. Princeton: Princeton University Press, 1982.

Barth, Karl. *Church Dogmatics*, vol. 1, 2. Translated by G. T. Thomson and Harold Knight. Edited by G. W. Bromiley and T. F. Torrance. Edinburgh: T. & T. Clark, 1956.

de Beauvoir, Simone. *The Second Sex*. Translated and edited by H. M. Parshley. New York: Vintage Books, 1974. Originally published as *Le Deuxième Sexe: I. les Faits and les Myths*, II. *l'Expérience Vécue*, in 1949.

Berg, Barbara J. *The Remembered Gate: Origins of American Feminism. The Woman and the City, 1800–1860*. New York: Oxford University Press, 1978.

Briffault, Robert. *The Mothers*. New York: Grosset & Dunlap, 1963. Originally published in 1927.

Caffarel, H., ed. *Marriage Is Holy*. Translated by Bernard G. Murchland, C.S.C. Notre Dame, Ind.: Fides Publishers Association, 1957.

Chodorow, Nancy. *The Reproduction of Mothering: Psychoanalysis and the Sociology of Gender*. Berkeley and Los Angeles: University of California Press, 1978.

Cixous, Hélène. "The Laugh of the Medusa." Translated by Keith Cohen and Paula Cohen. In *New French Feminisms: An Anthology*, edited by Elaine Marks and Isabelle de Courtivron. New York: Schocken Books, 1981.

———. "Sorties." Translated by Ann Liddle. In *New French Feminisms*, edited by Elaine Marks and Isabelle de Courtivron.

Collins, Sheila D. *A Different Heaven and Earth: A Feminist Perspective on Religion*. Valley Forge, Penn.: Judson Press, 1974.

Culler, Jonathan. *On Deconstruction: Theory and Criticism after Structuralism.* Ithaca, N.Y.: Cornell University Press, 1982.

————. *Saussure.* London: Fontana Modern Masters, 1976.

Daly, Mary. *Beyond God the Father: Toward a Philosophy of Women's Liberation.* Boston: Beacon Press, 1973.

————. *Gyn/Ecology: The Metaethics of a Radical Feminism.* Boston: Beacon Press, 1978.

————. *Pure Lust: Elemental Feminist Philosophy.* Boston: Beacon Press, 1984.

Derrida, Jacques. *Dissemination.* Translated by Barbara Johnson. Chicago: University of Chicago Press, 1981.

————. *Of Grammatology.* Translated by Gayatri Chakravorty Spivak. Baltimore: Johns Hopkins University Press, 1976.

Downs, Robert B. *Friedrich Froebel.* Boston, G. K. Hall, 1978.

Dreyfus, Hubert L., and Rabinow, Paul. *Michel Foucault: Beyond Structuralism and Hermeneutics.* Chicago: University of Chicago Press, 1982.

Duden, Barbara. "Das schöne Eigentum: Zur Herausbildung des bürgerlichen Frauenbildes an der Wende vom 18. zum 19. Jahrhundert." in *Kursbuch 47: Frauen* (March 1977).

Eisenstein, Hester. *Contemporary Feminist Thought.* Boston: G. K. Hall, 1983.

Eisenstein, Hester, and Jardine, Alice, eds. *The Future of Difference.* Boston: G. K. Hall, 1980.

Ellenberger, Henri F. *The Discovery of the Unconscious: The History and Evolution of Dynamic Psychiatry.* New York: Basic Books, 1970.

Feral, Josette. "The Powers of Difference." In *The Future of Difference,* edited by Hester Eisenstein and Alice Jardine.

Feuerbach, Ludwig. *The Essence of Christianity.* Translated by George Eliot. Introduction by Karl Barth. Foreword by H. Richard Niebuhr. New York: Harper and Row, Harper Torchbooks, 1957. Originally published as *Das Wesen des Christentums,* in 1841.

Fichte, Johann Gottlieb. *Addresses to the German Nation.* Translated by R. F. Jones and G. H. Turnball. Chicago and London: Open Court Publishing Company, 1922. This translation is based on Vogt's edition of Fichte's *Reden an die deutsche Nation* in the Bibliothek pädagogischer Klassiker, Langensalza, 1896.

Foreman, Ann. *Femininity as Alienation: Women and the Family in Marxism and Psychoanalysis.* London: Pluto Press, 1977.

Foucault, Michel. *Discipline and Punish: The Birth of the*

Prison. Translated by Alan Sheridan. New York: Vintage Books, 1979.

Freud, Sigmund. *An Outline of Psycho-Analysis*. Translated and edited by James Strachey. New York: W. W. Norton, 1949.

———. *Civilization and Its Discontents*. Translated and edited by James Strachey. New York and London: W. W. Norton, 1961.

———. *The Future of an Illusion*. Translated and edited by James Strachey. New York: W. W. Norton, 1961. Originally published as *Die Zukunft einer Illusion*, in 1927. This translation is based on the second edition, published in 1928.

———. *Totem and Taboo*. Translated and edited by James Strachey. New York: W. W. Norton, 1950.

Fröbel, Friedrich. *Mutter- und Kose-Lieder: Dichtung und Bilder zur edlen Pflege des Kindheitlebens*. In *Pädagogische Schriften*, vol. 3, edited by Friedrich Seidel. Vienna and Leipzig: A. Pichler's Witwe and Sons, 1883. English translation: Friedrich Froebel, *The Mottoes and Commentaries of Friedrich Froebel's Mother Play*. Translated and edited by Susan E. Blow. New York: D. Appelton, 1899.

Gallop, Jane. *The Daughter's Seduction: Feminism and Psychoanalysis*. Ithaca, N.Y.: Cornell University Press, 1982.

Gilligan, Carol. *In a Different Voice: Psychological Theory and Women's Development*. Cambridge, Mass.: Harvard University Press, 1982.

Hausen, Karin. "Family and Role Division: The Polarization of Sexual Stereotypes in the Nineteenth Century—An Aspect of the Dissociation of Work and Family Life." In *The German Family*, edited by Richard J. Evans and W. R. Lee. London: Croom Helm, 1981.

Hegel, G. W. F. *Phenomenology of Spirit*. Translated by A. V. Miller. Oxford: Oxford University Press, 1977. Originally published in 1807.

Hertz, Deborah. "Salonieres and Literary Women in Late Eighteenth-Century Berlin." *New German Critique* 14 (Spring 1978): 97–108.

Hoffmann, Julius. *Die "Hausvaterliteratur" und die "Predigten über den christlichen Hausstand."* Berlin: Verlag Julius Beltz, 1959.

Irigaray, Luce. *Amante marine de Friedrich Nietzsche* [Friedrich Nietzsche's Seagoing Lover] Paris: Editions de Minuit, 1980. Translated by Lillian S. Robinson. In Christian Faure, "Twilight of the Goddesses," *Signs* 7, 1 (Autumn 1981): 85.

———. "This Sex Which Is Not One." In *New French Fem-*

inism: An Anthology, edited by Elaine Marks and Isabelle de Courtivson. Translated by Claudia Reedev. New York: Schocken, 1981.

James, E. O. *The Cult of the Mother Goddess.* New York: Praeger, 1959.

Kilpatrick, William H. *Froebel's Kindergarten Principles Critically Examined.* New York: Macmillan, 1916.

Klein, Viola. *The Feminine Character: History of an Ideology.* London: Kegan Paul, Trench, Trubner, 1946.

Kojève, Alexander. *Introduction to the Reading of Hegel.* Translated by James Nichols. Edited by Allan Bloom. New York: Basic Books, 1969.

Kristeva, Julia. *Desire in Language: A Semiotic Approach to Literature and Art.* Edited by Leon S. Roudiez. Translated by Thomas Gora, Alice Jardine, and Leon S. Roudiez. New York: Columbia University Press, 1982.

————. *Powers of Horror: An Essay on Abjection.* Translated by Leon S. Roudiez. New York: Columbia University Press, 1982.

————. "Woman Can Never Be Defined." Translated by Marilyn A. August. In *New French Feminisms,* edited by Elaine Marks and Isabelle de Courtivron.

————. "Women's Time." Translated by Alice Jardine and Harry Blake. *Signs* 7, 1 (Autumn 1981): 13–35.

Kuhn, Annette, and Wolpe, AnnMarie. *Feminism and Materialism: Women and Modes of Production.* London: Routledge and Kegan Paul, 1978.

Lacan, Jacques. *Écrits: A Selection.* Translated by Alan Sheridan. New York: W. W. Norton, 1977.

————. *Speech and Language in Psychoanalysis.* Translated, with notes and commentary, by Anthony Wilder. Baltimore: Johns Hopkins University Press, 1981. Originally published as *The Language of the Self: The Function of Language in Psychoanalysis,* in 1968.

Lasch, Christopher. *Haven in a Heartless World: The Family Besieged.* New York: Basic Books, 1979.

Lindemann, Mary. "Love for Hire: The Regulation of the Wet-Nursing Business in Eighteenth-Century Hamburg." *Journal of Family History* 6, 4 (Winter 1981), pp. 379–395.

Makward, Christiane. "To Be or Not to Be ... A Feminist Speaker." Translated by Marlene Barsoum, Alice Jardine, and Hester Eisenstein. In *The Future of Difference,* edited by Hester Eistenstein and Alice Jardine.

Marenholtz-Bülow, B. von. *Gesammelte Beiträge zum Verständ-*

niss der Fröbel'schen Erziehungsidee. 2 vols. Kassel: George H. Wigland, 1876–1877.

Marks, Elaine, and Courtivron, Isabelle de, eds. *New French Feminisms: An Anthology*. New York: Shocken Books, 1981.

Martin, Biddy. "Feminism, Criticism, and Foucault." *New German Critique* 27 (Fall 1982): 3–30.

Marx, Karl. *Capital*, vol. 1. New York: International Publishers, 1967.

————. *Critique of Hegel's "Philosophy of Right."* Translated by Annette Jolin and Joseph O'Malley. Edited and introduced by Joseph O'Malley. Cambridge: Cambridge University Press, 1970. Originally published in 1844.

————. *Writings of the Young Marx on Philosophy and Society*. Edited and translated by Lloyd D. Easton and Kurt H. Guddat. Garden City, N.Y.: Doubleday, Anchor, 1967.

Mitchell, Juliet. *Psychoanalysis and Feminism*. New York: Vintage Books, 1975.

Neubauer, John. *Bifocal Vision: Novalis' Philosophy of Nature and Disease*. Chapel Hill: University of North Carolina Press, 1971.

————. *Novalis*. Boston: G. K. Hall, Twayne Publishers, 1980.

Neumann, Erich. *The Great Mother: An Analysis of the Archetype*. Translated by Ralph Manheim. Bollingen Series, vol. 47. Princeton: Princeton University Press, 1955.

Novalis, *Henry of Ofterdingen*. Translated by Frederick S. Stallknecht. Cambridge: John Owen, 1842.

————. "Klingsohr's Tale." Translated by Gordon Birrell. In *German Literary Fairy Tales*, edited by Frank G. Ryder and Robert M. Browning. The German Library, vol. 30. New York: Continuum, 1983.

————. *Schriften*. 2 Vols. Edited by Paul Kluckhohn and Richard Samuel. Leipzig: Bibliographisches Institut, A.G., 1929. Second edition, 3 vols. Stuttgart: Kohlhammer, 1960–1975.

O'Brien, Mary. *The Politics of Reproduction*. Boston, London, and Henley: Routledge and Kegan Paul, 1981.

Patai, Raphael. *The Hebrew Goddess*. New York: Avon Books, 1967.

Pestalozzi, Johann Heinrich. *How Gertrude Teaches Her Children: An Attempt to Help Mothers to Teach Their Own Children and an Account of the Method*. Translated by Lucy E. Holland and Francis Turner. Edited, with introduction and notes, by Ebenezer Cooke. 5th ed. London: George Allen and Unwin; Syracuse, N.Y.: C. W. Bardeen, 1915.

————. *Leonard and Gertrude.* Translated by Eva Channing. Boston: D. C. Heath, 1885. The German editions are *Lienhard und Gertrud. Ein Buch für das Volk,* 4 vols., Stuttgart: J. G. Cotta, 1819–1820; L. W. Seyffart, ed., 5 vols., Brandenburg: H. A. Muller, 1869–1870; F. W. Burgel, ed., 5 vols., Paderborn: F. Schoningh, 1903.

Preston, James J., ed. *Mother Worship: Theme and Variations.* Chapel Hill: University of North Carolina Press, 1982.

Rich, Adrienne. *Of Woman Born: Motherhood as Experience and Institution.* New York: A Bantam Book, 1977.

Rose, Hilary. "Hand, Brain, and Heart: A Feminist Epistemology for the Natural Sciences." *Signs* 9, 1 (Autumn 1983), 73–90.

Rowbotham, Sheila. *Woman's Consciousness, Man's World.* Harmondsworth, Middlesex, England: Penguin Books, 1973.

————. *Women, Resistance, and Revolution: A History of Women and Revolution in the Modern World.* New York: Vintage Books, 1974.

Ruether, Rosemary Radford. *New Woman, New Earth: Sexist Ideologies and Human Liberation.* New York: Seabury Press, 1975.

————. *Sexism and God-Talk: Toward a Feminist Theology.* Boston: Beacon Press, 1983.

Sanday, Peggy Reeves. *Female Power and Male Dominance: On the Origins of Sexual Inequality.* Cambridge: Cambridge University Press, 1981.

Schatzman, Morton. *Soul Murder: Persecution in the Family.* London: Allen Lane, 1973.

Schleiermacher, Friedrich. *Christmas Eve: Dialogue on the Incarnation.* Translated, with introduction and notes, by Terrence N. Tice. Richmond, Va.: John Knox Press, 1967.

Schreber, Daniel G. M. *Kallipädie oder Erziehung zur Schönheit durch Naturgetreue und gleichmässige Förderung normaler Körperbildung.* Leipzig: Fleischer, 1858.

————. *Kinaesiatrik oder die gymnastische Heilmethode. Für Ärzte und gebildete Nichtärzte nach eigenen Erfahrungen dargestellt* (1852). In Alfons Ritter, *Schreber, das Bildungssystem eines Arztes.* Inaugural Dissertation, Erlangen University, 1936.

Silber, Kate. *Pestalozzi: The Man and His Work.* London: Routledge and Kegan Paul, 1960.

Stanton, Donna. "Language and Revolution: The Franco-American Dis-Connection." In *The Future of Difference,* edited by Hester Eisenstein and Alice Jardine.

Stone, Merlin. *When God Was a Woman.* New York: Harcourt Brace Jovanovich, 1976.

Welch, Sharon D. "The Battle for Truth: Foucault, Liberation Theology and the Insurrection of Subjugated Knowledges." Ph.D. diss., Vanderbilt University, 1982.

Werner, Oscar Helmut. *The Unmarried Woman in German Literature, with Special Reference to the Period 1770–1800.* New York: Columbia University Press, 1917.

Index

Marilyn Chapin Massey is dean of the
School of Arts and Sciences at the College
of New Rochelle. She has taught at Munde-
lein College, the University of Louisville,
Duke University, and Harvard Divinity
School and was a Carnegie Faculty Fellow
at the Bunting Institute of Radcliffe College. She is the author of *Christ Unmasked:
The Meaning of Life of Jesus in German Politics*
and translator/editor of several works of
the writings of the Young Hegelians.